chibi Vampire
The Novel

2

STORY BY TOHRU KAI
ART BY YUNA KAGESAKI

TOKYOPOP®

HAMBURG // LONDON // LOS ANGELES // TOKYO

Chibi Vampire The Novel 2
Written by Tohru Kai
Art by Yuna Kagesaki

Translation - Andrew Cunningham
English Adaptation - Ethan Russell
Copy Editor - Peter Ahlstrom
Design and Layout - Jennifer Carbajal
Cover Design - Fawn Lau
Editor - Kara Stambach

Pre-Production Supervisor - Erika Terriquez
Digital Imaging Manager - Chris Buford
Art Director - Anne Marie Horne
Production Manager - Elisabeth Brizzi
Managing Editor - Vy Nguyen
Editor-in-Chief - Rob Tokar
VP of Production - Ron Klamert
Publisher - Mike Kiley
President and C.O.O. - John Parker
C.E.O. and Chief Creative Officer - Stuart Levy

A 🌀TOKYOPOP® Novel

TOKYOPOP and 🌀 are trademarks or registered trademarks of TOKYOPOP Inc.

TOKYOPOP Inc.
5900 Wilshire Blvd. Suite 2000
Los Angeles, CA 90036

E-mail: info@TOKYOPOP.com
Come visit us online at www.TOKYOPOP.com

ISBN: 978-1-59816-923-2

First TOKYOPOP printing: May 2007
10 9 8 7 6 5 4 3 2
Printed in the USA

CONTENTS

A lit match glittered in her fingers.

She watched the flame sputter under her breath and wondered if there was anything as powerful as fire. Everything ugly, everything dirty—if you burned it, it would turn to ash and disappear. Fire cleansed everything.

But it also burned away beauty.

Painful memories surged to the surface of her mind.

A life extinguished amid a raging inferno . . . that was why she had to burn everything.

She stood between twin rows of townhouses and let her gaze wash over the street. The newly gentrified neighborhood masked back alleys filled with garbage and clutter. Bicycles plugged gaps between garage sheds. Abandoned magazines and newspapers plastered the asphalt. There was no sense of community.

She knew nobody here cared about keeping the neighborhood clean. The families flocking to refurbished houses were only interested in themselves. Everyone was holed up in their domestic fortresses, eating dinner or watching television.

The street itself was empty.

She touched the match to a rolled newspaper. A moment later, the makeshift torch flared into life. She tossed the blazing paper onto a pile of magazines and slinked back into the shadows.

Bigger! Grow bigger and burn everything! Clean it all!

She suppressed a giggle before darting into the night. She wanted to stay and watch the conflagration, but that would never do.

She would have to wait for the post mortem.

An anxious reporter spat put rapid commentary into a live microphone an hour later.

"We're here live in Kamatsu-ku, where the Eighteenth Fire Brigade is battling the lethal blaze you see behind me. At least one home has burned to the ground, and officials are issuing warnings for the rest of the block."

Behind her, the fire blazed and crackled.

The reporter furrowed her brow in annoyance as the camera swung away to cover the inferno.

"Authorities have not speculated on the origins of the fire, although a string of similar incidents throughout Sanjou-shi have fuelled speculation about arson."

She continued her commentary for a little while longer and then concluded with "Reporting live from the scene . . ."

Onlookers drifted back to their homes as the broadcast ended, aware the fire was under control.

She left with them, her ankle-length skirt flapping in the evening breeze.

Ouch!" Karin Maaka dropped the piping hot tray on the kitchen counter. Twenty minutes at two hundred and thirty degrees meant that an iron cupcake tray was hot even with oven mitts on.

Karin whipped off the gloves and jammed both hands into her mouth, dancing excitedly.

"Are those for Kenta Usui?" A sniveling voice wafted in from the kitchen door. "Ain't puppy love sweet!"

"Aiieee!" Karin yelped. She hovered over the seven cupcakes like a bear protecting its cubs. "Knock it off, Anju! These aren't for him."

Karin's little sister stood in the door, clutching a doll in one hand.

"Can't fool us!" cackled the doll, its mouth flapping wide. "No summer classes today, so you decided to bake your way into Usui's heart. Ha ha ha!" The dummy held a plastic butcher's knife in one hand, a relic from a popular cartoon.

"Oh, grow up!" Karin snapped.

Anju innocently flicked her platinum locks. "It wasn't me. It was Boogie."

Karin thrust a toothpick into one of the cupcakes to make sure they were finished. She found Anju annoying, and Boogie even more so. Her little sister looked for all the world like an antique doll. But Anju offset that image by lugging Boogie everywhere she went, speaking through the dummy with a grotesque, cartoonish voice.

"And please try not to scream this early in the morning," Anju continued in schoolmarm tones. "Mama and Papa just went to bed. And so did I."

"Sorry." Karin hung her head. Her family were night owls—and for good reason. The members of the Maaka clan were vampires.

Karin alone toiled in the daylight. A recessive gene had left her immune to sunlight. And garlic, which came in handy for eating pasta. Unlike most vampires, Karin didn't need to drink blood to survive. Instead, her body generated *excess* plasma, which overflowed once a month to the point where she had to inject it into someone else to avoid disaster.

Anju stifled a yawn. "Why are you making cupcakes if they're not for Usui? Shouldn't you be studying?" Karin had failed most of her exams and had been sentenced to a summer of divided between classes and home studies.

"Maki got some cheap tickets to the Amusement Square. I thought I'd bring some snacks to save money."

"So Boogie was wrong," sniffed Anju. "He thought you were going out with Kenta Usui."

"Yes! Completely wrong! Why would I be going out with him?"

"I thought he was your best friend."

"Yeah, but not like *that!*"

Karin had actually known Maki Tokitou longer than anyone else, but for some reason shied from telling her the truth about the Maaka family. Kenta Usui was the only human to know the secret of her unusual condition. He was also the only boy she allowed to get close to her.

"We aren't dating or anything! Kenta is just a friend!" Karin folded her arms defiantly.

Anju glanced out the window. "Whoever you're going with, you should bring an umbrella," she said.

Karin moaned. "The weatherman said it wouldn't rain until this evening." But the sky was heavy with clouds and looked unlikely to hold back its payload much longer.

Suddenly, her ears perked up. A siren wailed past the window. A fire truck.

Karin and Anju exchanged meaningful glances. There had been a lot of fires recently, and the pattern seemed to be inching ever closer to their own neighborhood. The blazes were getting too close for comfort—especially since the media had started speculating about arson.

"Take care out there." Anju said, suddenly serious. "Days are long right now, and if something happens, none of us will be able to rescue you till after sunset."

Karin smiled as she popped cupcakes out of the pan. "Thanks. But the world really isn't as dangerous as you think it is, you know."

"Here you go. A little something for your last day." The old woman pulled a brown envelope from her apron pocket and presented it to Kenta Usui.

Kenta bowed low and accepted the gift, hoping he'd escape before she pinched his cheeks, the way old people do. A nearby golden retriever wrestled in vain with the leash tethering it to the woman's porch. The dog wanted nothing more than to play with Kenta a little longer.

"Taro really likes you," the old lady said. Her wrinkles doubled, and Kenta realized she was smiling. "You'll be first on my list for dog walker the next time we go on vacation."

"Any time!"

"Oh, such good manners! You turned out to be so much nicer than you look!"

Kenta stared at the woman, who continued to smile sweetly. "Um, thanks."

He stuffed the envelope into his satchel and backed away.

"Thank you for everything!" the woman cooed.

"You're welcome."

Kenta shuffled down the street. It was hard being a dog walker in July. The sun was setting, but it wouldn't cool off for a few more hours yet. Kenta had already been drenched in sweat before walking the dog because of his day job as a mover. But it was getting ridiculous. *At least the restaurant is air conditioned,* he reflected.

Kenta turned into an alley that served as a shortcut to his family restaurant, where he would work until closing. Summer was the time to make as much money as possible before school and studies ate into his time. But in the off weeks, he could work three jobs and dump the cash into the household budget.

Kenta lived alone with his mother, who often struggled to make ends meet. She had divorced young and had a child even younger, which meant that she was often the target of lecherous bosses. Her refusal to play along with their less than savory demands often earned her the enmity of her female coworkers, and more often than not her dismissal. Kenta frequently found himself paying the bills in a desperate inversion of the parent-child relationship.

Get good grades, graduate, get a good job. Look after mom.

A piercing shriek snapped Kenta out of his reverie.

"What are you doing?!"

Kenta found himself standing in a public playground. Two figures were struggling on the other side of a spidery jungle gym.

"Let go!"

"I just want you to tell me more! Isn't it a nun's job to spread the word of God?!"

"I'm just a novice! I have to get back to the convent!"

"I can drive you there, sister. We can stop by my house on the way."

"No! Let go of me!"

As Kenta edged closer, the figures resolved into an imposing businessman and a young girl in a white habit. The nun was on the verge of tears. The businessman had twisted her arm behind her back and was wrestling her toward a black sedan.

Kenta had read enough manga to know a kidnapping when he saw one.

"Hey! Let her go!"

The suited man bolted from the park at the sound of Kenta's voice.

Kenta gingerly knelt beside the nun. "Are you okay?"

The girl looked up with untrusting eyes as the sedan tore into the evening. She stepped away from

Kenta. A moment passed as the pair sized each other up. Finally, the nun bowed her head and muttered an awkward expression of gratitude.

She appeared to be about the same age as Kenta, fifteen or sixteen. Her face had the delicate features of a Kyoto doll. Long lashes and alabaster skin made her look all the more like a porcelain figurine.

She must have felt so helpless, Kenta reflected. The thought linked her to his mother's problems. *The restaurant can wait.*

"I was just passing by," Kenta offered lamely. "Are you hurt?"

The nun's face relaxed into a smile. "I'm fine. My name's China Oriska. I'm a novice from the Saint Christina Convent. Thank you for intervening like that."

"I'm Kenta Usui. Who was that man?"

China's expression clouded. "I don't know. He stopped me on my way home and asked about God. I tried to steer him to a priest, but he didn't seem interested in anything but his own vulgar impulses." She hung her head with shame. "What if he really did seek salvation? Maybe I've failed him."

Kenta could scarcely believe someone could be so naïve. The man had obviously wanted to force himself on China and used proselytizing as a pretext. "You were right to refuse," he growled. *Nobody tries to force a nun into a car for a spiritual chat.*

Something about the way China held her head make Kenta think of his mother once again. She was constantly navigating promises of promotion or job hunting based on whether or not she acceded to her various bosses' overtures. She never shared her problems with Kenta, but he always learned about them from the neighborhood gossips anyway.

It seemed even nuns faced the same problem. *Too many perverts in the city,* Kenta concluded. China's assailant had looked like any other businessman, rendered anonymous by neatly parted hair and a dark gray suit. Everything about him fit the stereotype, except for a shockingly loud red and yellow tie.

What kind of world do we live in where guys like that resort to kidnapping? Kenta smiled grimly at the omnipresent danger of metropolitan life. Just the other day his friend Karin Maaka had a run in with the yakuza. It seemed there was no escape.

And then it started to rain.

The drops spattered lightly against the asphalt. Kenta peered into the sky and tried to estimate how many seconds they had before the showers began.

"Uh oh." China hunched over to protect a square parcel. Kenta whipped an umbrella out of his satchel and handed it to the nun.

"Take it," he said.

"What about you?"

"I'll be fine. Gah!" Kenta suddenly realized the time. "I'm late for work!" He darted through the playground, fending off the warm rain with his satchel.

China watched him go from beneath her protective canopy. Her cheeks flushed the color of cherry blossoms as her voice slipped unbidden from her lips. "Kenta Usui . . ."

The umbrella was useless, filled with holes, but China didn't notice.

Karin had watched the exchange from the far side of the road, her legs rooted in place.

Maki had wanted to go shopping after visiting the Amusement Square, so the two girls wound up in an accessories store across from the park. They had been comparing purchases when Karin spied Kenta and a young woman talking in the playground. She couldn't hear what they were saying, but the timbre of the interaction unnerved her.

Who is she? Karin's mind raced furiously as she watched from across two lanes of traffic. *She's so pretty. Does he know her?* It wasn't until Kenta gave the newcomer his umbrella that Karin realized Maki was sheltering her with her own.

"Don't worry about it."

"Mind reader."

"She must be a nun. I know I haven't been to church since . . . ever, but I'm pretty sure nuns aren't allowed to date."

"I'm not worried."

"Uh huh. I'm sure she's just an acquaintance. Maybe a neighbor or a friend of the family."

"I said I'm not worried!"

"Okay." Maki watched the nun wander off.

Karin was grateful to Kenta for keeping her family's secret. Not every human would be cool with the knowledge that his best friend was a vampire. But she no longer had feelings for him, Karin repeatedly told herself. If Kenta had a girlfriend—even a beautiful nun—it was none of her business.

"Come on," she said finally. "I'm hungry. Let's find something to eat."

Maki chewed her lip, a dubious expression on her face. "Okay."

The girls walked along the street, huddled beneath a single umbrella. Two fire trucks sped past them with a gaggle of police cars in hot pursuit.

"Another fire?" Maki's eyebrows fell.

"Cops, too," Karin noted.

"The fire must be close. Look at all the lights on the next block."

"Should we check it out?"

"Nah," Maki said, looking at her phone. "It's already after seven. Let's go home and eat something."

Karin nodded her agreement. "If everyone stops to take a look, they'll just get in the way."

"At least it's raining. That ought to keep the fire from getting out of hand. The last one was right next to Mister Tsuchita's house. You know, the history teacher? He lives in Komatsu-ku."

"Really? Is he okay?" Karin had no idea who Mister Tsuchita was.

"He's fine," Maki said knowingly. "But the fire was so intense that he can't use any appliances for a while."

The conversation flowed to new subjects, but Karin still saw Kenta at the park in her mind's eye. She was aware of her heart beating loudly and hoped Maki wouldn't notice.

Calm down! Jeez. Get a grip, Karin. Seriously. You're acting like a dumb shojo *heroine who doesn't realize she's in love until the final episode.* Karin tromped obliviously through puddle after puddle, caught up in her thoughts.

I'm not in love. I'm so not!

But her mind kept returning to a vision of Kenta handing his umbrella to the pretty nun before running off with his satchel over his head.

Kenta is just a friend . . .

But that damn nun kept taking his umbrella.

Wind scattered the summer rain, leaving damp spots on the cinderblock wall.

China glanced out from under the ragged umbrella and felt her expression brighten involuntarily. An older nun was walking a few yards ahead of her, sheltered from the rain by nothing by a wimple.

"Mother Superior!" China squealed with relief as she dashed toward the new figure.

The older nun turned around. Silver-rimmed spectacles framed her thin, intelligent face. "Sisters do not *run,* my girl."

"I'm sorry." China slowed to a more pious gait. "I am so relieved to see you!"

Mother Superior peered over the rim of her glasses. "Relieved? Did something happen during your duties?" She noticed the ragged umbrella and wrinkled her nose. "Is that a *man's* umbrella?"

China averted her gaze awkwardly.

"Yes, ma'am. I was bothered on the way home and a boy stepped in before things got out of control. Such a kind heart—as if sent by the Lord in my hour of need."

"Good heavens! What . . . ? No. First let's get you inside."

The nuns had arrived just in time for the dinner gong. The Saint Christina Convent housed just seven nuns, with China as their sole novice. One of the older sisters was absent when the two women arrived in the dining hall.

"Sister Takeoka has a fever," explained one of the nuns as the newcomers sat. "Perhaps China can assume her duties." It was more a statement of fact than a question.

"Were you okay alone?" One of the other nuns interjected. China was decades younger than the sisters. While some took austerity to extremes, others doted on her like grandmothers.

"There was an incident on the way home," China said, her face clouding over.

"So you said." Mother Superior gazed at China with piercing eyes. "What happened?"

China described her misadventures to a chorus of distressed sighs and clucks from the other women.

"How awful!"

"She may be a novice, but she still belongs to God alone!"

"May the Lord have mercy on his soul."

"The outside world gets more dangerous every year."

The sisters were grave and ashen faced, not unlike the stone tableaux behind them. "It's not really so bad," China decided. "There are good people, too. One of them saved me. He gave me this umbrella so I wouldn't get wet."

China felt her face warm at the thought of Kenta. *He was so brave! The same age as me, but so tall. And his eyes! Did God send him to save me? I bet the martyrs looked as resolute when they were being persecuted. I should have asked for his address. How can I return his umbrella with that?*

"Are you coming down without something, too?" A plump busybody named Sister Yamashita rested a hand on China's arm. "You're not eating."

China began shoveling food into her mouth. "I'm sorry. Lost in thought."

The women retired to an alcove after dinner, offering prayers before a painting of the Virgin Mary. China clasped her hands and copied the other nuns' posture.

Mother Superior boomed an incantation. "I recognize the divinity of Christ, and give thanks for His merciful protection. Forgive my sins and accept the good that I have done."

The sisters repeated each refrain, heads hung low.

"Protect me while I sleep, and deliver me from danger."

The prayer sparked old memories for China. *I was asleep. And Got protected me from terrible misfortune. Probably.*

China was loath to doubt. It wasn't right. Not for a servant of God.

But that fire . . .

That fire . . .

"China!"

The sharp voice pulled China back to reality. The nuns had finished their prayers while she was lost in her reverie. Her cheeks flushed with embarrassment as China fumbled with a silent apology. But her gaze fell upon a collection of flickering candles and she was lost in thought once more.

China's parents had been pious folk, and her twelve years of schooling had been spent at Catholic academies for girls. Faith was a constant companion, and she had joined the convent to ensure a life of purity in the service of God.

"Ahem." Mother Superior peered imperiously over the rims of her spectacles.

China sank to the floor, her hands clasped in prayer. "I'm so sorry . . ."

"Say the Lord's prayer fifty times, and then come to my room."

"Yes, ma'am."

The other nuns filed out of the chapel, leaving China alone in front of the painting of the Virgin. "Lead us not into temptation but deliver us from evil." *O Lord, please help me. I love the convent. I want to stay here.*

She did, too. Mother Superior was stern yet kind. China adored chatty Sister Takeoka. Sister Yamashita could cook meals suitable for the angels themselves. Sister Uzawa was so sensitive she always seemed on the verge of tears. All of the sisters had time for an untrained novice and China loved them all.

Help me. Save me. Don't let me succumb to the weakness within me.

China prayed in earnest. She clamped her eyes tightly closed, so that she would not be bewitched by the candle flame.

"Hey everybody, I'm home!" Karin bounded through the kitchen and threw open the door to her bedroom. She found her brother slung in her desk chair, lazily focused on the television glowing in the darkness.

"Ren! What are you doing in here?"

"Shut up," growled Ren, absorbed in a baseball recap. "I'm watching TV. I'll get out of your way when the news is over."

Karin flicked on the overhead light to annoy him. Everyone else in her family could see in the dark thanks to their vampire genes. She alone required light to see. Maybe she was defective, but she didn't care. Light was better than dark. Dark was scary.

"I thought you were staying at your girlfriend's house tonight?" Karin pouted. The only television in the house was in her room, which meant that the rest of the family had to hunker down there if they wanted to watch anything. None of them had ever shown much interest, though. Karin was pretty sure she had never seen her brother watch the news before.

Ren stole a moment from the baseball coverage to glower at his sister. "I said, shut up."

The news switched to local coverage as Ren swung back around to watch.

"The latest in a series of blistering fires broke out at the Royal Villa Sanjo. Firefighters arrived at the blaze at a quarter of seven. A local woman was taken to the hospital after she was found on the scene bleeding from the head."

Karin and Ren exchanged worried glances. The Amusement Square was next to the Royal Villa Sanjo. Karin had been just blocks from the fire. She remembered the emergency vehicles racing past just after she had seen Kenta and the nun.

"The woman has been identified as building resident Minori Yokono, age twenty-eight. She's listed in stable condition with minor cranial fractures. The victim claims to have been struck after discovering someone starting a fire in the garbage. Police are investigating possible links to a recent series of fires believed to be arson. Next . . ."

"So it *was* Minori," muttered Ren. He turned off the television, as if this was the piece of news for which he had been waiting.

Karin gaped. "You're going out with the woman on the news?"

"Yeah. I went over there tonight like we planned, but there were cops and firefighters everywhere. I thought something might be going on so I hung out and did some eavesdropping."

"Well, it's a good thing we decided not to see what all the fuss was. We might have bumped into you." Ren ran through women like a cop goes through donuts. Karin made an effort to keep her friends away from him.

Ren slumped with relief.

"You can't just poke your nose in everywhere. You're not one of them," he admonished. "I took off once the crowd started talking about an injured woman. If I'd stayed around to see Minori, I would have just gotten mixed up in their little circus."

Karin couldn't imagine any woman wanting to be with Ren. It was just like him to cut and run when the going got tough. "Aren't you worried about her? The news said she cracked her skull! You should be in the hospital."

Ren glared at Karin as if she had suggested the grass was blue. "Retard."

"What?"

"You heard me, dumb ass. If I showed up at the hospital to check on Minori, the cops would be asking all kinds of questions. They're running around like headless chickens trying to find this arsonist. Anyone even remotely connected to the fires is going to get the third degree. You know what would happen if they find out I'm not human . . ."

Karin shuffled in the doorway. She knew Ren was right, but it didn't make her feel any better.

"So here I am." Ren threw his arms wide. "In a few days, the hospital will be crowded with her friends and family. I can go then. The cops and the press will have moved on to a new story. If anyone gives me grief, I can just wipe their memories."

Ren stood up to leave. "Don't you start pretending you're normal like the rest of them. You're defective. You can't even erase memories."

Karin threw herself on her bed once Ren stormed out. *Why does he always have to be so nasty?* Karin decided he only cared because his girlfriend was in the news. Seeing her name on the screen gave him vicarious fame.

She didn't know why he thought she'd put her nose in anyway. She didn't want anything to do with adventure. Just last month she had been kidnapped after investigating a series of assaults. Her mother and Anju had to save her.

My little sister!

Today had been Karin's one day off all summer, and it was almost over. Tomorrow would bring physics studies, and then a long evening shift at the family restaurant.

I think Kenta works tomorrow night, too.

Kenta had worked out a complicated schedule that included night shifts at Julian. That usually followed a day moving other people's furniture and walking other people's dogs.

Maybe he's there now.

Images of Kenta with the nun rushed unbidden into her mind.

Gah! It's none of my business!

Karin shook her head to clear her thoughts. *Why am I thinking about this so much?* She pulled open a drawer and began rummaging for pajamas.

That girl was pretty for a nun. She looked so pure and elegant. She did seem to spend a lot of time looking at Kenta, though.

The thoughts came back as soon as she pushed them away. Karin sighed.

Julian was bustling the next evening.

The family restaurant was always busy on Saturday nights, and things only got busier during summer vacation. The place was packed with lovers and families and singles, and the rumble of voices threatened to drown out the background music.

Kenta strode forward as a flock of customers walked in the door. "Welcome to Julian!"

Karin eyed him anxiously as she escorted a tray of *bento* boxes to a booth in the back. She reckoned Kenta had the false urgency of a ticket scalper. Was his mind on other things? He'd been acting unusual ever since he showed up for work. Greeting diners could be done on autopilot, but his heart clearly wasn't in it.

"Tandoori chicken curry and fresh tomato pasta, right?"

"No—fried shrimp curry and mozzarella balls."

"Right. Sorry. And two iced coffees with that?"

"Iced milk tea and hot coffee!"

Karin shook her head. Kenta usually had a good memory, to the point where he could successfully navigate the restaurant's ingredients menu to help diners with specific allergies. But tonight he couldn't even keep an order straight.

Karin scurried to the table before the situation escalated. "Excuse me. I'll take your order."

She wriggled an eyebrow to indicate that Kenta should slink away quietly. Her cheeks flushed as he passed. She could feel her pulse surge—the vampire side of her nature. She knew she had to keep her distance. But this was unusual. Her heart didn't normally beat so quickly when he was around. Karin wondered why.

"I should have gotten her number . . ."

The whisper made Karin's blood run cold. Kenta had been so relieved to have someone else take over that he started talking to himself.

He means that nun! Karin spun around to see what he was doing. But he was just clearing dishes off an empty table, his face bland with disappointment and regret.

That means they're not going out. He must have just met her if he doesn't even know her number . . .

Not knowing her number was clearly weighing on him. Karin could see it on his face. Her heart fluttered once again.

Not being able to see that nun again makes him this miserable?

The thought pricked at her heart like a thorn. She knew her vampire genes thrived on his

unhappiness, but this was something different. The usual butterflies had been replaced by a suffocating squeeze in her chest. She wanted to turn around and look at Kenta again.

What is this? A new symptom of my monthly blood rush? I've been noticing things ever since I realized my vampire instincts are triggered by others' unhappiness. That must be what's happening here.

Karin frowned as she shuffled to the kitchen with her table's order. *This is so embarrassing. I hate my body. It's like I'm in love with Kenta . . .*

Telepathy did not number among Karin's vampiric abilities. She had no way of knowing how far off the mark she was. Kenta *was* deeply troubled by something. But his thoughts were more prosaic than something as exotic as forbidden love.

His repeated thought was this: *How can I possibly afford to buy a new umbrella?*

Kenta has lent China his sole umbrella in a moment of sympathy inspired by memories of his mother's similar experiences. But he had already forgotten the name of her convent and had no way to contact her. More to the point, he didn't have the money for another umbrella.

Karin, of course, had no way of knowing any of this. She could see in his face that something was bringing him down, and as usual her worries said more about her than Kenta.

Are you . . . in love with her?

The thought ricocheted through her brain as her chest tightened.

Gah! Why am I like this? He can love anyone he wants to. It's got nothing to do with me! We're just friends! I don't have time to think about this!

"Who ordered the mushroom omelet in white sauce?" Karin surveyed the restaurant floor. Turnover was fierce on Saturday nights. Get 'em in and get 'em out.

A sharp cry from the front of the restaurant interrupted Karin's thoughts. A woman was fussing with her wailing baby. Karin rushed to the hostess podium.

"Is he okay?"

The woman hovered over the baby, cooing and shushing in an embarrassed attempt to make it quiet down. The other waiting diners were moving away from the commotion, and Karin realized the baby had vomited all over the floor.

Karin directed the mother to a restroom before grabbing a mop and bucket. When she got back to the foyer, Kenta was already rolling up the rug.

"We've got to send this out to be steam cleaned," he said, eyeing her cleaning supplies. "Wiping it down isn't going to accomplish much."

"Okay." Karin leaned on the mop anxiously.

"Thanks for helping me out earlier. I needed that."

"No, no . . . It was . . . Um . . ." Karin fumbled. *Why are you so out of it today? Does it have anything to do with that hussy? I heard you talk about her number. Well, I've got your number, buster.* Karin wanted to say all of that, but instead settled for a succinct, "No problem."

Kenta hoisted the rolled up rug over his shoulder, oblivious to his friend's troubles. "I'll take this out back. There's another one in the storage room, right?"

"Sure. I'll mop up."

Karin slapped the mop on the tile and swept it back and forth as Kenta walked away. She was too wrapped up in her thoughts to pay much attention to the waiting diners surrounding her. Eventually, Kenta returned with a fresh rug and her anxiety resurfaced.

"Karin, let me put this down . . ."

"Sure." Karin stepped aside to give him room and promptly slipped on the wet flooring. Kenta lunged forward and wrapped his arms around her. Tightly.

Karin's body temperature surged three degrees. Kenta's velocity sent the pair crashing onto the sensor mat by the automatic doors, which swished open. The overhead air conditioner puffed out a blast of cold air.

Karin opened her mouth to scream, but no sound came out. It was all she could do to keep breathing. *He's too close!*

Kenta was now lying on top of her, their arms entangled awkwardly. Karin could feel her pulse thundering ever faster. Her heart beat violently and her vision blurred. Karin feared her vampire instincts were kicking into gear.

The next sound drained the color from her face. "Kenta!"

Kenta twitched at the sound of his name. He managed to extricate his limbs and stand up. He craned his head to see who had spoken.

The automatic doors framed a pretty girl in a white habit. One hand held a black bag; the other covered her dainty mouth. Her cheeks were red with emotion. An older nun stood beside her. The elderly sister was equally mortified by the vision before her. "Oh my!"

Karin realized what the tangle of staff must look like to outsiders and color swiftly returned to her face. She launched to her feet.

"Kenta . . ." whispered the younger nun.

"China!" Kenta's mood instantly brightened at the arrivals.

Karin's heart skipped a beat.

China indicated Kenta. "This is the boy I was talking about last night at dinner, Sister Yamashita. He's the one who saved me."

Sister Yamashita bore down on Kenta like an elephant. "My word! Thank you so much, young man. You saved China! I'm sure the hand of God has brought us together."

"No, I just . . ." Kenta took two steps backward, looking around for an escape. His eyes alighted on Karin's vexed face. "Oh, Karin! This is Sister China. We met yesterday. Some guy was giving her grief and . . ." He laughed nervously. "The world sure is getting dangerous these days."

China smiled meekly. "I'm not a sister yet. Just a novice. Thank you again for helping me yesterday. I was going to return your umbrella, but I forgot to get your address."

As she spoke, China dug a small folding umbrella out of her bag. "I took it with me today just in case we ran into each other again. What a coincidence!"

Kenta took the umbrella with a huge grin, and Karin's heart skipped another beat. "Sorry it's just a useless umbrella," he said. The waiting diners look on with deteriorating patience.

Karin couldn't bear to watch any more. A new pain had beset on her, different from the earlier blood rush. It was a heavy, crushing feeling, the kind she usually got when Kenta was depressed.

"I'll put these away," she said, indicating the mop and bucket. "If you put the rug down, we can get back to work."

"Okay, Karin," Kenta said.

Karin could hear the nuns saying their farewells as she left. She looked over her shoulder and saw

Kenta waving goodbye. She watched him smooth the new rug over the floor and sighed. Her heart was still pounding, fast enough for her to feel it.

I was near Kenta too long this time . . .

Karin had traditionally only had to contend with her blood rush once a month. But recently, her timing was all over the map. She had no idea what was going on, but found herself forced to spew blood more and more often.

Ever since she had discovered that others' unhappiness triggered her vampiric instincts, she had grown far more empathetic. Most days she could sense if someone was down just by walking past them. Something inside her changed in their presence. Kenta was the worst offender.

The only way to deal with the overflow was to bite someone and inject her excess blood. Karin lacked many vampiric talents, including the ability to wipe her victims' memories. She usually relied on Anju to clean up her messes. But her little sister was exhausted from bailing her out so often.

Karin struggled to keep her instincts in check. Maybe she could trip and scrape her knee or get a nosebleed. Something to relieve the pressure. *Being a klutz can come in handy sometimes!*

But she was too timid to hurt herself deliberately. *This is what I get for being so close to Kenta! It was almost like we were hugging! In public!*

Sweat beaded on her brow at the thought. Karin slung the cleaning supplies into a cupboard. *Stupid!*

As she headed back to work she saw Kenta barreling down on her with the umbrella. He was lost in his own world, his usually grumpy face beaming.

"You look happy." It was more an accusation than a question.

"Those nuns are so nice!" enthused Kenta. "Look, they patched all the holes in my umbrella and sewed it back onto the spokes. I wish I could remember which convent they were from. I've already forgotten again."

"I think she said the Saint Christina Convent in Sanjo-shi."

"That's it! Thanks, Karin!" Kenta practically skipped back to the staff room.

How can he be so happy? A minute ago he was so depressed he could barely work . . .

Karin trudged to the nearest empty table and ran a washcloth over it.

China, huh? I guess she was kind of pretty. He seemed awfully happy to see her again.

The thought sparked a pain deep in her chest.

Neon lights and windowpanes glittered against the darkening sky. The days were long in late July, but the last vestiges of sun had already succumbed to the evening.

China scurried toward the main hall in quiet desperation. *I'm so late! I hope I don't miss evening prayer!*

She wasn't used to being out alone after dark. The sisters rose at four in the morning and slept at nine o'clock at night, which meant she had just minutes until lights out.

The nuns' lives revolved around their duties. Missionary work, community service and the like vied for their attention along with prayer and supplication.

China had spent most of the day volunteering at a retirement home with Mother Superior. The residents had been so happy for the attention, and after a few hours China had been left to entertain them on her own. Now she scuttled back to the convent in the darkness. Her footsteps echoed on the empty streets.

If something happens like the other night, there's no one like Kenta around to save me again . . .

She pictured his eyes, so like the piercing gaze of a martyr. At least, that's how China saw them. They were so soft and kind when she returned his umbrella.

China covered her mouth with a clenched fist—an unconscious gesture she made whenever she was unsure of herself. She reckoned Kenta already had a girlfriend.

Maybe that girl at the restaurant. *Of course he has a girlfriend. He's so brave and kind. Everybody loves him.*

Not that it matters to me, of course.

But she couldn't shake the image of Kenta and that girl tangled together on the restaurant floor.

What's wrong with me? Kenta is . . . I don't think of him that way! I can't! It isn't allowed. I'm a servant of God.

China shook her head to clear her thoughts. She wanted to be a nun. A romantic entanglement was out of the question. Kenta was just a new friend. A very attractive friend.

Our Father, who art in Heaven, hallowed be thy name . . .

China whispered the Lord's Prayer as she trundled toward the convent. She was determined to spend her entire life in God's service. The drive for companionship was a secular happiness. She should be happy that Kenta had found love. He had called the girl "Karin Maaka." If they were hugging in such a public place, then it must be true love.

She sure was cute, with those big eyes. Plenty of curves. She'll be a good wife. I should pray for their happiness before I go to bed tonight.

This new plan felt like a weight off her back. China hastened her pace, ducking into a dark shortcut between two apartment buildings. It wouldn't do to miss evening prayers.

She had only ventured a few paces into the alley when she saw two figures embracing beside a parked car.

Just like Kenta! Everyone is so shameless!

China tore her eyes away from the figures and dashed past the couple. But it was too late. She had already seen their faces.

The man was a scruffy guy in his twenties. China had never seen him before. It was the woman who interested her. The girl was the same one China had seen clutching Kenta just two days earlier in Julian.

China darted into the shadows to get a better look.

It was definitely the same girl. She was a little shorter than China, with a pretty face framed in a bob haircut that grew longer in the front.

What does this mean? Is she cheating on Kenta? Who is this guy she's making out with? She's betraying Kenta!

China couldn't bear to watch any longer. She stepped deeper into the shadows and clasped her hands to her heart. It was beating so hard she feared it might burst.

Hiding in the darkness, China failed to see the young man fall to the ground the moment they pulled apart. She never saw the bite mark on his neck or the twin fangs glittering between Karin's lips.

"Are you done yet, Karin?"

China only let her gaze return to the scene at the sound of an unfamiliar voice.

"Yep." Karin was leaning heavily on a lamppost. Her chest rose and fell with heavy breaths. The new arrival was bending over the fallen body.

Who is this new guy? Why is her other boyfriend on the ground? Is he bleeding?

The second man was touching the fallen boy's head, examining his wounds. He looked more annoyed than worried.

China had heard about pickpocket gangs that would send someone over to distract the victim while another member swiped his wallet. *Is Karin a pickpocket? Why aren't they calling for an ambulance?* The endless questions left her paralyzed.

The new man stood up. He was very tall, with odd platinum hair that hinted at green highlights beneath the sodium lamps. His scarlet eyes were flecked with gold. An outrageous silk shirt hung lightly off his frame. China reckoned he might have foreign blood running through him.

The man glowered irritably at Karin. "You should be better at this by now."

"Sorry," Karin answered him weakly.

"It took ages to clean up his memories. And is this really the best you can do for prey? Just look at this guy . . ."

"I'll be more careful next time."

"Next time?" he snarled. "You've gotta be kidding me. I can't believe Anju has the patience to look after you. I'm done."

"Gosh!" Karin sulked. "There's no need to be such a wenis. You're one to criticize, you horn dog!"

"Oh, shut up," he said, slapping her head.

China watched the conversation unfold with widening eyes.

How do they know each other? Why does she let this guy smack her around? Is he blackmailing her? What about Kenta? She looks so innocent.

China wondered how she could square this weak, almost innocent version of Karin with what she had seen moments before.

The man on the ground moaned suddenly.

The second man grabbed Karin and pulled her into the shadows.

The first boy hoisted himself by his elbows and looked around in a daze. Finally, he stood and wandered into the darkness.

As he passed, China heard him muttering in confusion about sleeping on the street. Eventually, he tottered out of view.

China was flummoxed. *I thought he was injured. Maybe they knocked him out with some sort of drug. They must be pickpockets if they're knocking people out. That guy did say 'prey' after all . . .*

China decided that whatever was happening with Karin, the other man was definitely up to something creepy. He was so tall and spooky . . .

A cell phone rang.

"Hello? Oh, Minori! Yeah, it's me, Ren." The silk-shirted man had adopted a syrupy voice at odds with the steely tone he'd used with Karin.

China risked poking her head into the light and was surprised to see Karin walking away from the scene. China wanted to run after her, and get to the bottom of things. She was sure there had to be a rational explanation for what she had seen. Karin seemed so nice. *I'm sure I'm missing something obvious.*

But Ren and his phone stood between them. If she went after Karin, China would have to run right past him. She was too frightened to risk it. Karin might be innocent, but this Ren character gave her a bad feeling.

"Sorry I'm late," Ren continued. "I had some stuff to take care of. I didn't forget! Minori! I'm heading to the hospital right now. Yes, I promise. Yeah, I love you, too. I was so worried."

Minori must be Ren's girlfriend, China reasoned. *Let me get this straight. Karin is going out with Kenta, but hugged the guy who just ran away, because Ren is blackmailing her . . . even though he's seeing another woman.*

Trying to puzzle out the relationships made China's head spin.

It's all so immoral!

China realized Ren was walking away from her, still chatting on his handset.

She followed him automatically, forgetting the convent. She had to figure out what was going on before something terrible happened to Kenta.

Ren was too engrossed in his conversation to notice China tailing him. He was some ways ahead of her already—partly because she was keeping her distance but mainly because she found it hard to keep up with his long legs.

Eventually, he snapped his phone shut and tossed it in a pocket. China was close enough to hear him muttering to himself. "God, I'm hungry. Maybe I should have a snack before I hit up Minori."

Ren turned a corner and headed toward a popular shopping district. China followed as he made his way down a narrow road crowded with carts and kiosks. Shoppers flowed in and out of stores like ants, dodging benches and lampposts and potted plants. A group of female students giggled to each other as Ren passed by. He cast a quick glance in their direction but didn't stop.

By the time China had reached them, the disappointment was evident on their faces. She sympathized. *He is awfully good looking . . .*

China knew she shouldn't be thinking such thoughts. Ren in particular had an edge to him, a dangerous aura that seemed to attract women like moths to a flame.

She didn't care for his flashy clothes, but his features were even, and there was a garnet flash in his long, thin eyes. The line from his cheeks to his chin, and the straight bridge on his nose showed his foreign blood. He looked as though he had just stepped down from the Saint Angelo bridge in Rome.

China was beside herself. *What am I thinking? This man is no angel!*

She had seen Ren in the alley, directing his arrogance and attitude at Karin. She had heard him on the phone, sweet-talking another woman. China wasn't convinced he hadn't used Karin as bait to steal money from the fallen man. It was blasphemous to compare him to an angel!

Up ahead, Ren suddenly perked up. A woman in a flared miniskirt stood a few meters in front of him. His eyes locked on her form as she bent over to adjust an expensive sandal. Patterned stockings traced their way up to the hem of her skirt. China watched as his gaze traced a path along them, like a hunter tracking his prey.

He's going to hit on that woman! On the way to meet someone he said he loves! It's so immoral! China stopped short. She didn't want to see what happened next.

I don't understand how Karin fits in. Ren must be ruining her! She helped him commit a crime. Maybe she's dating Kenta because his pure heart will save her! China mentally scribbled notes on an already complicated flow chart in her head. She decided that Ren was blackmailing Karin into helping him steal while Karin begged Kenta for help. *Okay, so it's a little complicated. It's just a work in progress.*

China watched as Ren made his introductions with the skirted woman. She knew she had to do something. Show him the penitent path, or at least warn his latest victim. But she was intimidated by his aggressive confidence.

"I found you!" A meaty hand grabbed China's arm and she almost screamed.

She whirled around in shock and found herself face to face with a familiar man wearing the same gray suit and flamboyant tie as the last time she'd seen him. Goosebumps broke out across her flesh.

"You came after me, didn't you?" It was the man from the park. His voice has the sugary cool of a predator feigning politeness. His black-rimmed glasses glinted in the colorful lights. He tightened his grip with a carnivorous claw. "A nun would never be in a place like this unless she was looking for something."

China recoiled in horror and disgust. "Stop! Let go!"

The man was far too strong for her to wriggle free, so she decided to shriek. "Help!" A passing woman stared at the skirmish in surprise but was quickly shooed away by the businessman.

"Come on," he cooed, dragging China to a dark corner. "We're in public."

China tried to plant her feet on the ground to no avail. "Help! Somebody!"

But everywhere she looked she saw only frightened women who lacked the strength to challenge her attacker. There was only one man in sight . . .

"Hey! Ren!" she blared. And just once, for emphasis, "Cheater!"

Ren was occupied with a greater crisis.

The skirted woman had looked amazing from behind. She radiated the kind of stress that triggered Ren's vampiric instincts, and also had good taste in shoes. But from the front she was a different story. When she turned to answer his greeting, Ren had done a triple take. She was like a five-course meal of ugly with a little extra ugly on the top.

"Me? Yes, I'm free!" she wailed in a grotesque parody of seduction. Her face had more lines than a singles bar. Ren reckoned she was as old as he was, without any of the benefits of being a vampire. She'd tucked her gray hair beneath a stylish wig and appeared to have applied her makeup without the benefit of light or focus.

Ren preferred blood with the sharp taint of stress. But it was imperative that his victims be women. This monstrous hag was something altogether different. No matter how stressed she was, he didn't like the thought of putting his mouth on those wizened jowls.

The woman was absolutely thrilled.

"What a catch! Fate must have brought us together. Are you hungry, or should we head straight back to my place and get to know each other a little better?"

Ren had never been happier to hear someone else screaming in sheer terror. He sprang into life at the sound of China's cries.

"Sorry," he called back to the crestfallen woman as he dashed off. "I thought you were my ex-girlfriend!"

A moment later, Ren found himself in an alley, confronted by the image of a suited man wrestling a nun into an idling van.

"Cheater! Help me!"

Ren did his second triple take of the night.

Ordinarily he might have left her to her own devices. But he felt overcome with a sense of philanthropy after escaping from the smitten crone. He sighed inwardly and put a hand on the back of the attacker's head.

The man's body stiffed as if electrocuted. A moment later he crumpled to the ground beside the van.

Vampires routinely manipulated memories to protect themselves from those they fed upon. The act temporarily scrambled human consciousness, which meant that it could also be used as an offensive weapon if Ren needed to quickly overcome an opponent.

The nun had been pushed into the back of the van and was now clutching the doorway in shock. She kept shifting her eyes from Ren to the man on the pavement and back.

"Are you okay? Can you stand?" Ren took her arm and helped China out of the van. She blinked dumbly. Before she could speak, the silence was interrupted by a love-struck wail.

"Wait!"

The old woman hobbled nimbly down the alley, arms outstretched. "If you mistook me for an old girlfriend, this must be fate!" The clatter of her shoes on the pavement offset the puckering sound of her air kisses.

Ren felt the blood drain from his face. He grabbed China's arm in a panic.

"Run!"

Ren and China darted onto another street, weaving through the crowd to enter another alley. They kicked over a row of bicycles and cut through an empty building in an attempt to lose their pursuer.

China had no idea what was going on, but it was exhilarating. She held the long skirts of her habit with one hand and kept pace with her cheating rescuer.

Finally they reached a red stoplight and paused for breath. There was no sign of either of their attackers.

Ren regarded China out of the corner of his eye. He had planned to throw her into the old woman if she managed to catch up to them, and was impressed it hadn't come to that.

"Thank you," China wheezed, hands on her knees. It hadn't been easy keeping up with Ren. "You saved me!"

He regarded her dispassionately. Ren had internally analyzed China the moment he saw her. It was sheer instinct at this point. She looked fit enough beneath that shapeless habit, and she had a nice face. But at sixteen, she was too young even for him; and the religious thing was a turn off.

"My name is China Oriska. I'm from the Saint Christina convent." She bowed her head slightly and thanked him again. Maybe she had misjudged him after all.

Ren made a face.

He wasn't afraid of pious folk like some vampires he knew. Holy water and crucifixes only held power for those who believed in them. For Ren, they were just empty symbols of a venerable fairy tale.

Ren frowned. China radiated none of the stress he would have expected from someone in her position. *That* at least would have made her somewhat appealing.

He'd had bad luck finding someone to feed on ever since the arson that had put Minori in the hospital. He was starving. Drinking the blood of a panicked woman would have been wonderful about now.

Ren briefly debated feeding on the sour blood of a calm individual or waiting until he saw Minori. But even at this desperate hour, China looked so unappetizing. On the other hand, his girlfriend's stress was a beautiful thing. On top of her recent wounds, Minori had the ongoing stress characteristic of all women working for companies that viewed their female employees as glorified tea makers. Rising workloads as businesses slimmed down during the recession made her blood even spicier.

Ren hadn't seen Minori for three days. Just imagining how good her blood must taste was enough to get his vampiric instincts twitching.

The light turned green and Ren stalked off without another word.

"Wait!"

China hurried across the street to catch up to him. "I thought you were a cheating horn dog!" she cried.

Ren nearly tripped hearing those words come out of a nun's mouth.

"Shut up and mind your own business!" he snarled.

China flinched. "Sorry. I didn't mean to hurt your feelings. I just want to know . . ."

Ren waived her off imperiously. "Look, no offense, but you look like a pain in the ass. Go home before that guy finds you again."

China's face turned white at the thought of running into her attacker again. She hadn't bothered to pay attention during their flight and wasn't entirely sure how to get back to the convent.

The green light turned yellow and Ren quickened his pace.

China stood on the other side of the street and watched until he was out of sight. Traffic had started backing up and her habit was inspiring funny looks from the passing drivers. She headed back the way she came, lost in thought.

He didn't seem so bad. Could he really be a cheater and a thief? But he saved me. And his profile is so angelic. He held my hand!

China felt her cheeks turn red at the memory. Her eyes were wide with excitement. *Being a nun is more difficult than you would think,* she reflected.

I just don't know. Ren. Are you a good person? Or . . .

You're so late!" Minori laughed despite the accusation. "Keeping me waiting all this time. They'll only let you stay here until eight o'clock, you know." She flashed a coy smile from her perch on the hospital bed. "But I'm so glad you came!"

Ren fidgeted in a chair beside the bed. "You look happy."

"I am! Although it turns out fracturing your skull is a bad thing. But they're not putting a cast on it. I don't even know how they would do that. Anyway, it's just a small fracture. It doesn't even hurt as long as I don't touch it. They're keeping me here just in case my head splits open during my sleep or something. Who knows? But I'm getting out the day after tomorrow."

Ren stared at her blankly. Minori carried on, unperturbed.

"I have to take another week off of work and just hang out at home while I recover. The doctor's giving me a note so my boss can't complain. He stopped by for a visit, by the way. My boss, not the doctor. Well, the doctor stops by too, of course. But my boss said they can't get anything done without me. The work is backing up. He promised to get some temps in to help me out when I get back. That's good to know!"

"Wow. That's . . . great." Ren wondered how she could get so much out without coming up for air.

"Yep. And I was on the news, right? Everybody keeps popping in to see me. People are crawling out of the woodwork after seeing me on TV. Ha ha!"

Ren offered a sympathetic laugh, shoulders slumping. He couldn't believe it. Minori's stress was completely gone! She had been so delightful at first. Overworked and swamped with overtime, her blood had tasted wonderfully sour. But her hospital stay had somehow become a vacation. She was surrounded by friends and even her boss had lavished her with praise.

This wouldn't do at all.

Ren no longer wanted to drink her blood.

She was perfect three days ago! I'm starving!

He had gone so long without nourishment that he was more unwilling than ever to settle for bland blood. He needed to find a victim. Somebody in the prime of her life and crippled with stress. No men, children, or crones for him.

"What's wrong, honey? Bad mood?" Unexpectedly, Minori had finally stopped talking long enough to notice her boyfriend's glum expression. She peered at his face inquiringly. They were close enough to kiss, but Ren couldn't be less interested.

But of course he wasn't going to tell her that. "I was thinking about the arsonist," he gambled. "I'm glad you weren't seriously hurt, but he still hit you in the head. He'd better hope I don't get my hands on him!"

No sooner had the words left his mouth than he heard sirens. He could see nothing unusual from the hospital window, but it sounded like another fire had broken out.

"They better catch that guy soon," Minori shuddered. A surge of fear chased the energy from her face. The terror of her attack was fresh on her mind no matter how comfortable she got at the hospital.

"You told the cops about the arsonist, right? They'll find him soon."

"But I didn't see his face!" Minori wailed. "He was hidden by the hood of his parka. Once I realized it was the arsonist, I panicked. I was too busy trying to get away to get a good look at him."

"You didn't get any clues at all?"

"The only thing I can say for sure is that he was wearing a blue parka with dark gray pants and black leather shoes."

"A blue parka and gray pants?" Ren was dumbfounded. He didn't know anyone who could pull off that combination.

Minori nodded enthusiastically, pleased to have pulled Ren into a conversation. "And not casual pants, either. Slacks. Or pants from a suit. They really clashed with the parka, that's for sure. The cops think it might be a businessman who uses the parka to hide his face. Can you imagine setting things on fire and then calmly going in to the office?"

"A thin parka could fit in a briefcase," Ren reasoned.

"Sure. The guy was about my height in heels. Me in heels, obviously. Not him. He had an average build but looked awfully solid. He hit me with a bicycle pump. I could have died!"

"Yeah." Ren stood up decisively. "I shouldn't make you talk too much since you're still recovering. I should get out of here and let you rest."

Ren swept through the hospital's night entrance a few moments later. Emergency workers in orange overalls were manhandling a woman on a stretcher. He caught a snatch of frenzied conversation as they passed off the stretcher to the resident EMTs.

". . . inhaled high temperature smoke and her throat is swollen. Third degree burns on her right leg . . ."

"Tell the ER to get ready for a tracheotomy."

It was obvious the patient had been pulled from the latest fire. Nobody had died yet, but it was only a matter of time. The arsonist must have started twenty blazes by now.

I bet the arsonist tastes pretty good. I've heard serial killers are often motivated by stress. It's got to be stressful starting a fire when you know the cops are hot on your heels.

The thought intrigued Ren, but he had no idea how to track the arsonist down and no interest in feeding on men. He pushed the thought out of his mind and ambled toward the shopping district. He was sure to find a pretty girl there.

Another ambulance tore into the parking lot as he left, screeching to a halt in front of the ER entrance.

That evening was unusually slow at Julian.

The staff was generally rushed off their feet with the night crowd, but about once a month, an eerie silence would descend upon the restaurant and leave the employees with nothing to do. A few customers were engrossed in their laptops or canoodling with partners, but for the most part, the wait staff just hung out by the kitchen without much to do.

"Maaka, how late are you working?" Kobayashi sauntered over to where Karin was sitting.

"Six thirty. I swapped with Ishiguchi."

"It's ten after six now," Kobayashi said. "Why don't you go ahead and take off? We don't have any customers. Anyway, you've got a visitor."

Karin looked up and saw a girl in a white habit loitering by the front door. It was China.

"I don't think it's about missionary work," Kobayashi said.

Karin was perplexed. "She wants to talk to me? Are you sure it's not Kenta?"

"She asked for you by name and then pointed you out."

Karin looked around for Kenta. It had to be some kind of practical joke. But he was nowhere to be seen. When she remembered that he wasn't working today she only got more confused. What could the sister want?

Karin waved to China and then scurried to the staff room to change out of her uniform. When she caught up with China, the young nun was sitting on a bench in front of the restaurant staring wistfully at the night sky.

The plain habit only made her more radiant, Karin decided. China had long lashes caressing the biggest eyes Karin had ever seen. She carried herself with a rare grace.

It must be hard for her, being a nun. So restrictive! I guess boys are drawn to clean-cut girls, though. Kenta looked so happy to see her the other day. Karin hesitantly sat down beside China.

"Sorry to keep you waiting," she said. "You wanted to speak to me?"

China turned to face her with surprising gravitas. "My name is Oriska China. Um . . ." She steeled herself and tightly shut her eyes. "Karin, please stop betraying Kenta!"

Karin had no idea what she had been expecting China to say, but this certainly wasn't it. "Huh?"

"If you have a lover as wonderful as Kenta, you shouldn't go out with other people!"

"Um . . ."

"I saw you! In front of the Sakura Doori apartment building! I saw you hugging another man!"

Karin hadn't been expecting this, either. Her face was so hot she feared it might catch fire. She was sure her skin had turned as red as a brick. The accusation was embarrassing, but more to the point she needed China to pipe down in front of her work.

"Stop! Settle down! We need to go somewhere and talk about this."

Karin grabbed China's hand and led her to another bench a few blocks away.

The girls were sitting in front of a small baseball park between several high-rise apartment buildings. The area was always empty at night even though it bustled with activity during the day. They could have a sensitive discussion here without fear of being overheard.

"There's been a misunderstanding," Karin said, breathing heavily beneath a bank of flowerless wisteria. She was out of breath from dragging China here.

"You and Kenta are dating, right?" China was also panting. "I saw you at the restaurant the other night. I saw you hugging."

"No way!"

"And last night I saw you at the Sakura Doori apartments! You hugged another guy and then he collapsed."

Karin froze. *She saw me bite him!*

She couldn't speak.

China would never accept the truth, even if Karin could articulate it. She and Kenta hadn't been hugging, of course. He had merely caught her when she tripped. The incident triggered her blood rush, and so last night she and Ren went out to inject someone.

How much does she know?

She started to panic. Her warm blood chilled. She could feel it in her skin.

China simply stared at her feet. "I thought maybe you hurt the other guy you hugged, because he fell down. But he got up and ran away."

"No, he wasn't hurt. It was an accident." Karin didn't know what to say. She suddenly realized that China kept saying "hugged" instead of "bit." The nun seemed oblivious to her vampiric nature.

The realization made her relax. Perhaps too much, since she had just let slip an admission that it had been her in the alley.

China looked at Karin sadly. "You already have Kenta. Why would you cheat on him like that? Is that Ren person threatening you?"

Karin stiffened again. *Did she see Ren erase that guy's memory? How can I talk my way out of this?*

China regarded Karin wistfully. "I saw him yell at you and hit you on the head. Is he threatening you? Does he know some sort of nerve pinch or something?"

Karin was dumbfounded. It was too good to be true. China seemed on the verge of talking herself out of this whole scenario.

"I've read about it in books," China continued, oblivious. "Kung fu and things like that. Ren did the same thing when he saved me."

"Saved you?" Karin was so delighted to shift the conversation onto a new subject that she decided to overlook her brother's uncharacteristic heroism.

"Yes. Some guy was trying to push me into a van and Ren knocked him out. He didn't even ask for anything in return. I refuse to believe he's a bad person . . ." China trailed off.

Karin regarded China with suspicion. The nun hung her head as if remembering something painful.

"He called the man who fell over 'prey,' " she finally whispered. "Did he take his money? Did he force you to help him commit crimes? And then I saw him talk to one girl on the phone and another on the street. He's a womanizer."

Karin wanted to nod vigorously in agreement, but didn't. Ren was worse than a womanizer—he was a serial monogamist who barely gave women enough time to fall for him before dumping them. But she refused to speak ill of her family in front of a stranger.

The two girls sat in silence for a few minutes. It was China who spoke next.

"Karin, what do you think you're doing? Ren or Kenta . . . You should never date two men at the same time, no matter the reason."

"But I'm not dating them!"

"Please don't betray Kenta Usui! He has such a kind heart. Don't make him suffer!"

"Hang on! You've got it all wrong, China!" Karin hovered precariously on the edge of the bench. "I'm not dating them! Ren is my brother!"

"Your brother? He looks nothing like you . . ."

Karin sighed theatrically. "Ren looks like our mother. I look like my grandmother. Honestly. I'll bring my little sister along next time and she'll tell you. Or you can just ask Kenta yourself. He's met Ren before."

Karin was surprised China didn't immediately die from embarrassment. The nun had turned bright red and was covering her eyes with dainty hands.

"I can't believe it! I've been so rude!"

"And one more thing," Karin added, warming to her theme. "I'm not dating Kenta. We're just friends. When you saw us at the restaurant, I had tripped he caught me. It was embarrassing for everyone, trust me."

"Really? I just assumed that anyone embracing like that in a public place must be lovers. I even said a prayer for your future together!"

"Stop!" Karin shrieked. She was on the verge of hysterical laughter. Or was it tears? *Maki, Anju, and now this girl. Why does everyone think we're together?*

"I'm not going out with Kenta! We live near each other and go to school together and work at the same restaurant. That's all! I thought he and you were . . ."

China looked astonished. "Kenta and I? What about us?"

"Um." Karin was embarrassed just saying it out loud. "It seemed like he liked you or something. I thought . . ."

She realized how ridiculously jealous she sounded and shut up. China didn't seem to notice and plowed on ahead.

"He's a very kind person. Don't you agree?"

Karin recalled everything Kenta had done for her since transferring to her school. He hadn't even rejected her once he discovered that she was a rare breed of injecting vampire. He had kept her secret, and done his share of mopping up spilled blood.

"Yeah," Karin said, meeting China's gaze. "He's a good guy."

Karin relaxed at the sight of China's guileless smile. *She really does think Kenta is just a friend. She's not turning red like she was before! She—wait a minute! Why* doesn't *she think Kenta would be my boyfriend?!*

"Are you okay?"

Karin realized she had wrapped her arms around her head in frustration, then sheepishly lowered them. "It's nothing."

A thought struck her. China hadn't turned red when she mentioned Kenta . . . but she definitely did when she mentioned Ren. She had a bad feeling about this.

Before Karin could continue with that line of thought, China grew suddenly anxious. She cast around, sniffing the air.

"Do you . . . Do you smell something burning?"

Karin noticed it, too. The thick, acrid smell of burning plastic.

A fire! Karin's thoughts turned to the serial arsonist and she sprang to her feet. "Let's go see!"

"It's too dangerous!" cried China, her pale face turning even whiter. She grabbed Karin's hand and tried to anchor her to the spot.

Karin was taken aback, but there was no time to argue. She followed the insidious odor to one of the apartment towers. Karin rounded the building and ran straight into a wall of violent heat.

A pile of bicycles and tricycles by the side of the building had been doused with kerosene and set ablaze. Their seats and tires were on fire, creating oily columns of black smoke. The unmistakable stench of burning rubber turned Karin's stomach.

But the ghostly scene was nothing compared to what was in front of it.

Karin saw a figure in a blue parka watching the combustion with silent glee. He was so wrapped up in his psychosis that he hadn't noticed Karin rounding the corner. She instantly knew he was the arsonist who had set the inferno in motion.

He was too calm. If he had arrived on the scene by accident, he would have called the fire department or made a move to put it out. He wouldn't stand watching, laughing to himself.

Karin thought of Minori and remembered the fractured skull she had received as a reward for stumbling on the scene. She didn't want to be bashed with a bicycle pump. She fished a hand into her pocket to find her cell phone and quietly walked backward.

But grace was one of the many skills absent from Karin's repertoire. Her shoe caught on a rock and she tumbled to the ground with an undignified squeal.

The arsonist spun around, startled. The low-slung hood obscured his face, but he looked afraid of being caught anyway.

Before either of them could respond, China ran forward. She froze when she realized what she was watching. She let out a piercing wail so loud, Karin was convinced she could patent it and sell it as an ambulance siren.

"Help! Fire! Somebody help me! It's so hot! I'm scared! Help! Noooo!"

"China?"

China fell to the ground in anguish. She curled into the fetal position.

"China! What's wrong?" Karin leapt to her feet. But before she could check on her new friend, she felt an icy stare at her back.

She spun around and found the arsonist advancing on her. He withdrew a knife from one pocket, the blade gleaming orange in the firelight. "Why did you have to come here?!" he snarled in a high, hoarse voice. He slashed at the girls with a mixture of anger and panic.

China was huddled on the ground. Karin couldn't run and leave her behind. She decided the novice had the right idea and started screaming for help.

The arsonist was nearly upon them when one of the flaming bicycle tires exploded under the heat. Bits of burning rubber rained down on the assailant. Other pieces slammed into the side of the apartment, finally making enough noise for residents to open their windows.

"Fire!"

"The bikes are burning!"

The residents' cries temporarily stunned the arsonist. Karin seized the chance and yanked China to her feet.

"Run!" She hauled the girl away from the scene as quickly as possible, terrified that the arsonist would follow.

 ## CHIBI VAMPIRE AND THE
ARSONIST'S IDENTITY

Karin lost track of how long they had been running. Each time her legs threatened to fail her, she would picture the arsonist's gleaming knife and press on. Finally, her body gave out on a pedestrian overpass. Karin and China collapsed against a wall and held their legs.

"I think he's gone," China said, panting.

Karin took in their surroundings, which appeared to be free of maniacs in blue parkas. She flopped down on the edge of a red-brick flowerbed and buried her face in her hands. Her body temperature felt as high as the fire's. "Good. We got away . . ."

China sat next to her, and the two girls spent the next several minutes recovering their breath.

The sun had set several hours ago, and the city bloomed with neon lights and illuminated windows.

China was the first to speak. "Thank you, Karin. If you hadn't been there, I don't know what would have happened." She held her hands; they were still trembling.

"China . . ."

"I'm afraid of fire," the girl continued. "Terrified. When I see flames, my body just shuts down. I get too scared to move. It's too hot, too scary. I can't bear it."

Karin regarded her companion. The girl wasn't crying, but her long lashes were fluttering. Her skin was pale and the hairs on her arms were standing upright. Her patina of elegant grace had given way to the terrified fluttering of a scared child.

Something terrible must have happened to her, Karin thought. She threw an arm around China, despite the heat.

"It's okay," she said. "It's okay. Don't worry, China. Nothing's burning here. I'll look out for you."

China took a few deep breaths and then beamed with gratitude. "I know. Thank you." An embarrassed smile played across her mouth. "I was in a fire in kindergarten," China explained. "I've been afraid of it ever since. I can tolerate a match or a candle, but . . ."

"It's okay. Anyone who was in a fire probably feels the same way. It's nothing to be ashamed of." Karin rubbed China's back soothingly. They had become unlikely friends in an incredibly short time.

"Thank you," China said. "You're a good person, Karin. Just like Kenta. You two are very much alike."

"It's just a misunderstanding," Karin murmured, but China didn't hear her. The novice adjusted her wimple absently.

"It started during lunch. I was taking a nap. But the noise and heat woke me up. There was fire everywhere, and all the kids were screaming. A few of them died of carbon monoxide poisoning. I almost didn't make it myself, apparently. One of the teachers carried me out. Just like you saved me today."

"I didn't save you." Karin smiled awkwardly. "We just ran away."

Karin wore a clouded expression. "China, did you see the arsonist's face?"

China shuddered and wrapped her arms around her body. "No. I didn't see much of anything. The fire . . ."

"That's okay. You don't have to remember." Karin hugged her to stave off another attack of the shakes. She decided to change the subject. "Where are we, anyway?"

She wandered to the edge of the pedestrian walkway and squinted at the deepest concentration of neon lights. "I think that's the Amusement Square over there. Wow. That means we must have run a few miles!"

Fear had distorted their sense of distance. She never would have guessed she was a few wards over if she hadn't seen it herself.

"It must run in the family," China quipped. "I ran a long way with your brother last night when he saved me from being pushed into that man's van."

Karin knew that China must be feeling more secure if she was already joking. "China, my brother is dangerous. He's a sex fiend who treats women like toys. You need to be careful with him."

Unlike most vampires, Ren was very specific about the gender of his prey. And he would only drink from women whose blood matched his preferences. His womanizing was almost instinctual.

"You mustn't fall for someone like that," Karin warned.

"No way!" China protested. "He's much too scary! Oh. Sorry. I shouldn't call your brother scary."

"It's okay. He is."

"Anyway, I am a servant of God. To fall in love with a man . . . even one with such a beautiful face . . . He looks like the statue of an angel."

Karin cocked her head dubiously. China was digging a deeper hole.

"My brother is no angel," she said cautiously.

"I know. But he was so nice to me. I'm grateful. That's all." China made her denials while sporting reddened cheeks.

Karin was not convinced.

China had seemed flighty when she'd borrowed Kenta's umbrella the other day. She was positively swooning whenever the subject turned to Ren, even though he was obviously a womanizer. Karin knew the girl was in training to be a nun, but could China really be so naïve?

"China, have you ever been to a co-ed school?"

"No, of course not. Always Catholic girls' schools."

"Yeah, I thought so," Karin said.

"After I graduated, I asked to become a novice sister. My father objected at first, but my mother talked him into it." China put her hands together as if praying. "All my life, people have been saving me. Whenever I find myself in danger, someone is there. Kenta. Ren. You."

The sudden intimacy embarrassed Karin. Before she could say anything, China had brought the conversation back to the scene in the alley.

"You never told me what you and your brother were doing yesterday when I saw you," she said, frowning. "Why did you hug that guy? Was Ren making you do something criminal—maybe like distract that man so Ren could steal his stuff?"

China stared at Karin with equal parts worry and reprimand.

Karin swallowed, wordlessly. *We weren't stealing anything! But how can I explain that to her? I can't tell her we're vampires. She may be a novice, but she's still from a church with a lot of crosses!*

Karin knew China had seen the guy fall down after Ren had wiped his memories. She didn't think the sister would fall for the old "he was scared of a caterpillar" trick. She would have to lie her socks off.

"To tell you the truth . . ." she began. But before she could get any further a familiar voice rang out.

"Karin! China?" Kenta stood on the sidewalk below the overpass, looking up with astonishment.

"Um," Karin responded dumbly.

"What are you doing out here, Kenta?" China shifted uncomfortably.

"I'm on my way home from the moving company. Why are you two out here so late . . . together?"

"Late?" China glanced up at the darkened sky with shock. She had completely forgotten about the convent in her adventures. "Oh, no! I was only allowed out until the evening meal! I have to go!"

China hoisted her skirts up and took off toward the other end of the pedestrian walkway. She was much too panicked to worry about getting an answer out of Karin now.

"China!" Karin exclaimed.

"Don't worry, I know the way! Goodbye!" China bobbed down the stairs just as Kenta came bounding up the other set.

"Where did China go?" Kenta looked around in confusion.

His eagerness to see the sister made Karin feel as if her heart would burst. *Did he come all the way up here just to talk to her?*

Karin knew China wasn't allowed to see Kenta as anything more than a friend, but he was under no such restrictions. *Why do I keep thinking about this?! What do I care?!*

"China had to get back to the convent. It's past her curfew. I hope she'll be okay. I think we got away from the arsonist, but . . ."

"Arsonist?"

"Yeah. We saw him at the apartment buildings near Julian. He came at us with a knife. It was horrible!"

"Seriously?" Kenta asked with alarm. "The police didn't drive you home?"

Karin knew she had forgotten something. "We didn't tell the police!" she wailed. The fact of the matter was that once she had seen the blade, Karin couldn't think of anything else but running away.

Kenta was appalled. "What were you thinking? Did you at least call the fire department?"

"Well, when we ran away all the people in the complex started shouting about the fire. So I'm pretty sure that's taken care of." Karin climbed down from the pedestrian bridge. As she and Kenta walked into the night, she told him the whole story. Most of it. She left out exactly why China had come to see her.

"So you didn't see the arsonist's face?"

"Nope. He had this big hood. But I remember he was wearing a blue nylon parka and gray slacks. They didn't go together very well."

"Gray?" Kenta soured.

"What? Do you know something?"

"Did I mention how I met China?"

Karin wondered whether to tell Kenta that she had seen them, but decided against it. "She said you saved her."

"Right. Someone was trying to kidnap her. Just some normal-looking businessman. You would never expect a guy like this to come after you. Anyway, he wore a gray suit."

"Really?"

"Well, there must be thousands of guys in the city wearing gray pants, but . . ."

As if to prove a point, they walked past a small huddle of businessmen, half of whom wore gray slacks. As they passed, Karin remembered something important.

"Hang on," she said. "When you loaned China your umbrella—was it Friday?"

She already knew the answer. Kenta must have given China the remains of his umbrella shortly after saving her from the man in the gray suit. Karin remembered that a fire broke out not too long afterward and a woman was attacked.

This latter information surprised Kenta, who had been too busy working to watch the news. "What if it's the same guy? What if the guy who tried to snatch China was frustrated and so went somewhere else and started a fire?"

"Exactly!" Karin squealed. "What did the man you saw look like? Maybe we can identify him for the police!"

Kenta scratched his chin. "He had black-rimmed glasses. Neatly parted hair. Not fat but not very thin, either. Maybe late thirties? Less than seven feet tall. He kind of looked like every other businessman."

"So he was taller than me and China but shorter than you. That sounds like the guy we saw at the apartment complex. We didn't see his face, but there was a reflection in his hood that could have been from glasses."

Kenta gestured toward a red police box hanging on the other side of the next intersection. "We should probably tell the cops about this, Karin."

"Yeah, I guess so."

"Right. There's a police box over there. Let's call right now. I don't know if the guy who tried to kidnap China is the arsonist, but we can tell them both of our stories and maybe they can figure it out."

"Okay." Karin froze as she remembered something important. *What if the police want to know why China came to the restaurant, or what the two of us were talking about? I can't explain that in front of Kenta!*

Karin got dizzy just thinking about it. "Wait! We should really talk to China about this first! Bring her along with us!"

Kenta regarded her with uncertainty. "Yeah?"

"Yeah! I need time to organize my thoughts. Let's do it tomorrow. Please?"

"I guess that would be okay. It's not like you got a good look at him or anything. There's not a lot the cops can do with that information. Everything seems to revolve around China anyway, so we should probably get her involved."

Karin beamed with delight. "I'll call her as soon as I get home. I'm sure the convent is in the phone book."

"So just straight home for now, huh?" As Kenta spoke, a dull rumble from his stomach nearly drowned out his voice. The two friends trudged on in an embarrassed silence.

"So," Karin eventually ventured. "Are you eating enough?"

"There wasn't much time for lunch today," he offered. But his eyes sold him out, broadcasting a message that read: *I'm lying. I never eat lunch.*

Karin could always use a few extra bucks herself, but she knew Kenta was in an even more precarious financial situation. She was never short on meals, but it looked like her friend was too hard up to buy lunch. Karin had been bringing him lunch for so long that she hadn't realized he *needed* her to. When he had found out about Karin's family earlier in the semester, Ren had threatened to wipe his memories if he told anyone. The lunches were her way of apologizing.

But the lunches had trailed off in the summer. They only really saw each other at Julian. They got free meals there, so Karin never needed to make him lunch. She wondered if he actually ate on the days she didn't see him.

Was he really too busy to stop and eat? Or is he skipping meals to save pennies? Karin didn't have much time to worry about budgeting concerns, especially when one of her friends was working three jobs and still had to skip lunch.

The two friends lived on the same hill. Karin's family lived in a large house at the top, while Kenta had a small one-room apartment at its base. They were separated by less than eight feet. She contemplated dropping off lunches on her way to summer school but realized he would be mortified to received charity in front of his mother.

Karin grew warmer as she grew more agitated, and now she felt like she might spontaneously combust. She fanned herself wildly.

"What's wrong, Karin? Got a fever?" Kenta took Karin's hand, concerned.

The action sent her pulse roaring instantly. Her heart rapped out a staccato rhythm, as if she had just finished a triathlon. Even fleeing the arsonist hadn't created a response like this. Karin took a sharp breath.

"Oh! Sorry!" Kenta dropped her hand and stepped back a pace. She had explained once that her vampiric instincts triggered a blood rush when he got to close. He was beginning to be able to see the signs. "Are you okay?"

"I think so," Karin said hoarsely. She had just bitten someone the day before! She felt like she could never relax.

Karin glowered at two passing girls, who had mistaken her red face for the flush of young love.

"How cute! Puppy love is always so awkward!"

"We were that innocent once. Those first few dates are the best. Just the sight of each other's face gets your heart beating."

We aren't dating! Karin railed silently. *We're not! My heart is beating like that for a different reason!*

She spun on her heel, turning her back to Kenta. "I'm sorry, Kenta. It's my blood. I'd better go home!"

Kenta watched her stomp off into the night. "Don't we live in the same direction?" he muttered. He had much longer legs than she did. Karin had to power walk to stay ahead of him.

Whenever she looked back, Kenta was trailing thirty feet behind. She crossed the road, wandered through a park, and navigated a series of shopping streets, but the distance between them never changed.

Just because our houses are in the same direction doesn't mean we have to walk at the same speed. Maybe I should hurry up? I'm too tired to run. Why doesn't he have the manners to duck into a convenience store or something. He doesn't need to be so close!

Karin felt her heartbeat rising steadily. She knew it was rude to ignore him like this, but why did he have to follow her? It wasn't until she was nearly home that Karin figured it out.

"Bye, Karin. You should be safe this close to home, but be careful."

Oh.

Kenta had already popped through the fence that cordoned off his apartment. Karin realized he had been making sure the arsonist hadn't followed her, and keeping far enough away so that he wouldn't trigger another blood rush. He'd been worried about her.

Embarrassment washed over Karin. "You stupid girl!" *I kept wishing he would consider my feelings, but I never noticed his!*

Karin slapped her face repeatedly as she climbed the hill.

"Playing alone again?" Anju asked.

"Everyone in the family knows you're stupid. There's no need to advertise!" Boogie chimed in.

Karin froze. Her little sister was leaning out a window by the front door, the talking dummy in her arms. Karin had given Anju plenty of material for her favorite pastime—making fun of Karin. Unable to think of a witty comeback, she bolted through the door and crashed into Ren.

"Karin! Watch where you're going!" he snapped.

She whipped a hand to the wall and felt around for the light switch. But her cuff had gotten caught in one of his shirt buttons, which popped off with the rapid movement. The plastic bead bounced on the hard floor.

"You idiot! Now I'll have to get that fixed!"

"I'm so sorry!" Karin wailed.

"I was going out, you retard! Fix it now!"

"All right!" She rushed into her room, threw her bag on the bed, grabbed her sewing kit, and came running back. Karin would rather be boiled alive in a vat of lava than cross her brother when he was in one of his moods.

Ren hadn't stopped complaining while she was gone. ". . . and you know what else is wrong with you? You can never relax!"

"I'm sorry!" She threw herself onto a sofa and began affixing the offending button. "Oh, this sleeve's coming off, too. The thread's unraveling."

"Then fix it! Don't make me ask."

"Okay . . ."

Anju was mysteriously absent, which meant that Ren had been like this all evening. Their parents were probably out hunting, so there was no one to save her. Karin pushed a needle in and out of the buttonholes and considered her options. *I don't understand why he's so angry. Didn't he see Minori yesterday? He should be full now. Maybe he was too busy saving China to get to the hospital.*

China! Karin knew she had forgotten something. She continued sewing but decided to take a gamble and speak to her brother. "Thanks again for erasing that guy's memories last night."

Ren snorted. Karin decided the lack of yelling was a good sign and pressed on. "I heard you had an incident with a nun last night. A girl named China?"

"You know her?" Ren raised an eyebrow. "I was running away from some hag and found a guy trying to have his way with her. I pretended to save her in order to get away—you know, use her as a shield in case that old biddy caught up with me."

"You didn't drink from her?"

"She had no stress!" Ren snapped in disgust. "She was scared, but it's just not the same. That's the problem with religious types. They're too certain of things to have stress. Even though she was almost kidnapped!"

"Kidnapped!" Karin yelped. She pricked herself with the needle in surprise. Luckily the wound wasn't deep enough to draw blood.

"Be careful when you're sewing my things," barked Ren. "You'll hurt yourself."

"I know . . ."

"If you get blood on my jacket, you're buying me a new one."

Karin knew his clothes would always be more important to him than her fingers. She decided to try again. "The guy who was messing with China—was he wearing a gray suit?"

"How did you know?"

"It was him!" Karin breathlessly explained what Kenta had told her, and about the arsonist who had attacked her and China earlier that evening.

Ren studied the ceiling thoughtfully. "So you think the arsonist and the nun snatcher are the same person. Minori said something about a blue parka. He could easily carry it around in a briefcase. His height and weight matched the guy I saw."

Anju had quietly wandered into the room once Ren's tone had softened somewhat. She perched herself on a chair next to Karin and decided to weigh in. "It's not out of the question. What did the man you saw look like?"

"I didn't see his face very closely. Just an ordinary guy. Late thirties. Black hair. Gray suit. Florescent tie."

The kernel of a thought percolated in Karin's mind. Something didn't fit. The tie was an usual detail, and the arsonist could well have been wearing one beneath the parka when he attacked her. Kenta mentioned an outrageous tie as well. But the bubble popped before it coalesced into a meaningful theory.

"What about you, Karin? His face may have been hidden, but you saw something, right?"

Karin stopped sewing and tried to remember. She had only looked at him for a moment, and in a panic, so her memories were hazy. The arsonist had kept his hood pulled low, exposing on the lower half of his face. But when the tire exploded, he'd leapt sideways in surprise . . .

"Oh! There was a red mark under his chin. Like a birthmark. About this big." Karin held two fingers to her throat to indicate the spot's size and position.

"He can hide that as long as he keeps his head down," Ren said.

"It won't help us find him," murmured Anju.

"Well, this *is* Karin. What did you expect?"

Both her siblings shrugged.

"Hey!" Karin said, sulking. "I shouldn't have even tried."

"The man you saw wasn't hiding his face," Anju said to Ren. "Did he have a birthmark?"

"I don't know," he answered. "I'm not into checking out guys' faces."

Anju absently ran her fingers through Boogie's hair. "Everything points to the arsonist and the gray-suited man being one and the same. You two should be careful. Maybe he's after that nun because she saw him start a fire. Maybe she saw the Royal Villa Sanjo fire on Friday."

"China didn't say anything about that."

"Maybe she doesn't actually know she saw it. What if he had just started the fire and was taking off his parka in the shadows just as China walked by? She may have just thought he was a regular guy taking off his jacket and not paid any attention. But he might think she's on to him."

Karin had to begrudgingly admit that Anju had come up with a plausible scenario. "You're so smart! That makes perfect sense!"

"Yep. But don't get too excited. If that's what happened, then the arsonist later saw you with China. He might think she told you everything. And that means he thinks you're a threat. He could be coming for you next."

A chill ran down Karin's spine. She was barely stronger than a normal girl her age. As far as vampires went, she was useless. Coming up against a killer was more than she had in mind for the summer. Anju was right—the arsonist *had* gotten a good look at her.

Even worse, the apartment fire was very close to Julian. If the killer decided to search the area for her, he was sure to run into her at the restaurant.

"What should I do?" Karin wailed, looking from her brother to her sister and back. They had to clean up enough of her messes already, but this was no time for pride.

"Your best chance at safety is for the police to arrest the arsonist," Anju pointed out dryly. "We don't know who this guy is, so there's nothing we can do." She emphasized *we* in a tone of voice that indicated a supernatural solution. "All we can do is go to the police."

"The police?" Karin still feared a blunt discussion about China and Kenta.

"If it was just you, it might not matter. But the arsonist attacked you when you were out with China. You're a witness. It would be suspicious to keep quiet in any event."

Even Ren could see the sense in what Anju was saying. But it was clear to his sisters that he did not like the situation. He glared at Karin with undisguised venom. "What did I tell you? Don't stick your nose where it doesn't belong!"

"Scolding her now won't help," snapped Anju.

Karin shot her sister a grateful look. She didn't want to go to the police by herself, and knew there was no way Ren was going to go with her. But her sister might. She decided to risk asking.

Anju flatly refused. "What planet do you live on where a high school student needs to bring her younger sister with them? Besides, it's supposed to be sunny tomorrow. I can't go outside."

"Oh, the weather . . ." Karin slumped back on the sofa. She finished sewing the button on Ren's shirt and bit off the remaining thread.

"Finished?" Ren ignored her dejection and held out a demanding hand.

"Yeah."

Ren snatched the shirt and strode toward the door. "I'm going to find something to eat. I might not be back tonight, so warn the parents."

"Good luck."

Ren rolled his eyes. "You're a big girl. Don't dump all your problems on Anju." And with that he left.

"Why does he always pick on *me?*" Karin grumbled, slumping over on the coffee table.

"Ren didn't eat yesterday," Anju explained.

"I thought he went to see Minori in the hospital."

"Well it turns out that being in the hospital has been something of a vacation for her, so all her stress vanished. That's why Ren's in such a lousy mood. I think he blames the arsonist."

"Speaking of the arsonist, I guess I'd better call China and talk about going to the police." Karin gathered up her sewing kit and retreated to her room.

"Karin!" Anju called after her. "When you go to the police, try and make it as close to sunset as possible. We can't come after you until then if you get into trouble. I'll send the bats to keep watch. If the questioning gets uncomfortable, just try to drag it out until after dark."

Anju was alluding to attempts to fingerprint Karin or take a blood sample. Anju or Ren could alter the memories of any policeman who discovered more than he should, but once hard evidence was in the system, the family would be exposed.

"I'm sure it won't come to that."

"Just in case. Minori already gave them a description of the arsonist, so they'll know you're not a suspect. I doubt they'll take fingerprints, but even so."

"Thanks." Karin closed the door to her bedroom and flopped down on the bed. She took out her cell phone and dialed the operator. Eventually she got a number for the Saint Christina convent. The line rang about fifteen times, and just as Karin began to worry that the sisters would be asleep already, an old woman's voice answered the line.

"China? You must mean Oriska. She's reciting the Lord's Prayer at the moment. She was told to do so one hundred times, so it might be a while before she can speak on the phone."

Karin didn't want to risk her message getting lost before it got to China. "This is important! China and I saw someone starting a fire today. We need to talk to the police and give them a description of the arsonist so they can stop these killings!"

"How terrible!" the nun on the other end of the line said. "But it is also important for China to finish her prayers before socializing."

Karin was ready to unleash a torrent of very unspiritual language, but before she could, she heard a quiet discussion on the other end of the line and a new voice spoke.

"Excuse me. My name is Ryoko Toga. I am Mother Superior here. I understand you need to speak with China about an urgent matter? What exactly is it, may I ask?"

The mother superior sounded calm and efficient. Karin was sure she would understand. She explained how she and China had seen the arsonist and run away, and that she was calling to arrange a trip to the police station to report the crime.

"This explains a lot about her odd behavior recently," the nun said. "She begged me to let her go out today to speak with a friend. And she's had trouble with punctuality this week. Your situation sounds most dreadful. Please hold on a moment."

The mother superior vanished from the line, only to be replaced by China a short while later. The girl had never considered that her attacker and the arsonist could be the same person and was astonished to hear Karin's theory.

"It's not impossible," the novice said skeptically. "But I'm not sure. They weren't wearing the same clothes, were they? The person who started the fire . . ." China's voice broke off with a quiver as she thought about the fire.

"Don't think about that now!" Karin interjected. "Just tell me you'll come to the police station with me, and I'll handle the rest."

China agreed, and the girls made plans to meet at Julian the next evening. The police station was close to the restaurant. Karin figured they would get more mileage out of the police if China wore her habit, and meeting in the evening meant they would have backup from Ren and Anju if necessary.

Karin hung up the phone and fell backward on her bed. She heaved a long sigh of relief. Once they told the cops everything they knew, it would only be a matter of time before the arsonist was behind bars. The police would take care of everything. *I'm so tired I could fall asleep right now,* she thought.

But there was too much to do. Karin forced herself to hop up and shuffle out of the room.

CHIBI VAMPIRE
AND THE MYSTERIOUS
ABANDONED BULDING

Y ou're meeting her today at six?" Kenta asked in surprise, glancing at the clock on the wall as he cleared the table. The hands were pointed at a quarter to one. The lunch crowd had already left and Julian was almost empty.

"Yep. I get off then," Karin explained. "Can you come with us? You saw the man who tried to kidnap her, after all."

"I'll be here for another fifteen minutes, but then I'm working for the movers until late," he said apologetically. "But it's not like I saw the arsonist. It might be the same guy, but that's just a theory. I think you and China should be enough. The station is just around the block, so you should be safe together."

His use of the word *safe* made her cheeks turn red. *He's always helping me!*

Karin glanced around the restaurant. She had cleared the last dirty table and suddenly realized she had nothing to do.

"Kenta! Wait!"

"Huh?"

Karin rushed to the staff room. She grabbed a paper bag from her locker and came back to the main dining room. She awkwardly handed the bag to Kenta.

"This, uh . . . This is in place of the lunches I gave you at school!" she blurted.

Kenta took the bag, perplexed.

"It's to apologize for causing so much trouble. Ever since summer school started I haven't made any. But, um . . ." Karin trailed off lamely. She wanted to tell him it was bad to skip lunch; that the bag was a reward for walking her home last night—a dozen other explanations that fought to make it out of her mouth.

The bag was filled with cookies she had baked the previous night.

Karin had wanted to give him lunch as thanks, but he got a free lunch from Julian. He only needed meals when he was working at the movers. But she only ever saw him at the restaurant, so it was pointless to bring lunch then.

She had made cookies because she couldn't think of anything else that would last long enough for him to eat on the job. She knew cookies were too sweet to call lunch, but it was better than nothing.

"Anyway, these should be fine for the next three days," she said, arm extended.

Kenta's faced brightened at the thought of food.

"Oh! You shouldn't have!" The statement was a formality. Kenta was desperate to find out what was in the bag.

"They're cookies," Karin explained.

Kenta was just about to take the bag when the men's locker room door swung open. A rotund man in little round spectacles waddled out.

Karin and Kenta froze. The manager always had time to scold his employees. But instead he smiled at them with a far-off look in his eyes, as if reliving fond memories. "A hand-baked gift? Ah, young romance!" He clapped a stubby hand on Kenta's shoulder and then breezed into the dining room.

"It's not like that!" Karin yelled after him.

"Totally different!" Kenta agreed.

The manager ignored their cries. "Don't worry. I won't tell a soul. When you can pull yourselves apart, come back to work."

The manager left an awkward silence in his wake.

Karin decided to end it as quickly as possible. "It's just a replacement for the lunches I used to make you at school! Don't worry, I made some for China, too!"

That was true. Anju had caught her in the kitchen again, so she had to whip up a second batch of cookies to avoid another round of taunting from Boogie.

Karin was sweating despite the air conditioning. She was certain her face was red again. It had been turning red with alarming regularity these days. Her pulse beat rapidly. It wasn't just the intensity of her blood rush. Mental disharmony could affect her physically. If she remained near Kenta for much longer, her vampiric instincts might go off.

"I'd better get back to work!" she shrieked, and ran away.

But even in the dining room, her heartbeat failed to slow.

By six that evening there was no sign of things cooling down.

Karin changed out of her uniform and went out the back door, screwing up her face as the heat clobbered her.

I hope the police station has air conditioning, she thought, looking around for China. There was no sign of her in the parking lot or on the sidewalk.

"Karin Maaka?" A stern voice rang out from a black sedan parked on the side of the road. An older nun peered out the driver's window. Karin had never seen her, but she recognized the voice.

Karin strode over to the side of the car. "Are you Mother Superior?"

"Yes," the nun replied, pushing her glasses up the bridge of her nose. "My name is Toga. China explained the situation to me after you called. If one of our members is being chased by a criminal; I can hardly allow her to go out alone. I agreed to drive you both to the police station. Please get in."

Karin opened the passenger door and slid into the car. The station was just around the corner, but walking under the baking sun was a much less attractive prospect than an air-conditioned car ride.

She was surprised to see her new friend asleep in the back seat. "China!"

"Shhh!" The mother superior put a finger to her lips. "She must have finally been able to relax after sharing her burden. She fell asleep the moment she sat down. So many frightening things have happened to her recently. I want her to get as much rest as possible. We'll wake her when we get to the station."

The nun looked frosty, but Karin felt herself warming to her. Or maybe it was just the heat. Karin wiped a hand across her damp black bangs.

"I'm sorry," the mother superior said. "There is no air conditioning in the car. It was passed on to us as a charitable donation."

"That's okay. I'm used to it."

The car wheeled into traffic. The mother superior regarded Karin out of the corner of her eye as she drove. "How do you know China? Were you friends in school?"

"No, we only just met. We don't really know each other that well . . ."

The nun rose her eyebrows in surprise. "Really? And only yesterday you saw someone starting a fire and were assaulted by the arsonist! That must have been frightening. China was so grateful to you for saving her. I want to thank you as well."

"It was nothing . . ." Karin frowned. She peered uncertainly out the window. "This isn't the way to the police station."

"The arson investigation is under the jurisdiction of the Sanjo-shi precinct, apparently. I called the police as soon as I learned about your incident yesterday, and they told me to go over there. If we went to the local station they would just make us wait until the head detective got there."

That made sense to Karin, so she sat back in the vinyl seat. The setting sun was in her eyes. "How long will it take?"

"About fifteen minutes." The nun drove for a moment before speaking again. "I can not believe your parents allowed you to go to work alone today. You were just attacked! Did they think a child could take care of herself?"

"Oh, I haven't told them about it," Karin said nonchalantly. Even if she had wanted to, she hadn't had the time. Vampires were nocturnal creatures, and Karin's odd daytime cycle meant she rarely saw her parents. She was asleep before they got home from wherever they went, and they were in their coffins before she woke up.

But she couldn't explain that to a stranger.

The mother superior kept her eyes on the road, smiling faintly. The light of the setting sun glared in her spectacles. "You kept it secret? Maybe you were trying to keep them from worrying. It's not good to hide things, you know. I'm sure your parents love you very much."

"Yeah. It's just that my parents got home late last night," Karin bluffed. "I was going to tell them everything when I get home tonight."

"Oh, good. There are so many parents these days that never think about their children."

Not my parents, Karin thought. They tended to tease their children rather than spoil them, but their parenting was fundamentally sound. They did a good job looking after her. But there was no way she could reveal their true vampiric nature to the mother superior of a convent.

The car drove north, into an aging industrial part of town characterized by brick warehouses. Other cars would occasionally pass by, but Karin didn't see any pedestrians anywhere. Karin had unrolled the window to catch some air, but now dust and smog wafted in. She clamped her mouth shut, preferring to breathe the filthy air than roll up the window and risk turning the car into a sauna.

This is a funny place for a police station, she thought. *Aren't they usually near a town hall or train station or someplace like that?*

The southern side of Sanjo-shi was home to an amusement park and several shopping centers, so Karin had been there many times. But she knew little about the northern part.

The mother superior spoke again. "China mentioned something about the arsonist and the man who tried to kidnap her being the same person. What made you think that?"

"It was just an idea. When I told my brother and sister what happened, we thought maybe—"

"You spoke to your siblings?"

"Yep. We realized that the man who tried to kidnap China and the person we saw setting the fire had the same body type. And they were both wearing gray pants . . ." Karin trailed off again. She was overlooking something. She knew it.

"Is that all?"

"No—the kidnap attempt occurred very close to one of the fires. That's what made us wonder if they were the same person."

The mother superior looked doubtful. "It's an interesting theory," she said, emphasizing the last word.

The car started up a slope. The incline was gentle but long, and the mother superior was constantly shifting gears. Karin caught a glimpse of her boot stamping on the clutch. It was black and masculine-looking.

The nun interrupted Karin's thoughts. "I don't believe they are the same person. The motives for arson and kidnapping are quite different."

"My sister said China might have seen the arsonist changing out of the parka he used as a disguise."

"Oh, very good," the nun said, smiling faintly. "You're very lucky to have siblings you can talk to about these things. It sounds like a very nice family. Very nice."

The mother superior smiled; the glint of the sun off her glasses made her look calm. "You have such a good family, and yet you're more interested in spending time with boys. So naughty, dating several at once!"

"Huh? No, I'm not! One of them was my brother, and the other . . ." It sounded like China had glossed over a few details, accidentally giving off the wrong impression.

The mother superior carried on forcefully, ignoring Karin's attempts at correcting her. "That behavior is unacceptable. China also lacks the proper mindset to become a nun. She never makes curfew. She drifts off in the middle of prayer. Thinking of boys, no doubt. It simply will not do."

Karin noticed her heart was beating faster. In fact, it had been pattering for several minutes now. *Is this a blood rush?*

She started to panic. *Not now! I just bit someone two days ago! I shouldn't have any excess blood!*

Yet she could clearly feel her heart galloping in her chest. It was gentle but insistent— impossible to ignore.

But why? The only people with me are China and this nun.

Her vampiric instincts were triggered by other people's unhappiness. Just yesterday, her brother had been complaining that deeply religious people never really got stressed out, even in dire circumstances. Both of Karin's traveling companions trusted their souls to God's will. *Can they ever be truly unhappy?*

Karin turned and looked in the back seat.

China was sound asleep. A strong, warm wind blew through the open window, buffeting her cheeks. All three passengers swayed as the car took a curve. But while her faced twisted and a faint moan escaped her lips, China did not wake up.

Karin spun back around in her seat. *I don't care how tired you are, nobody sleeps like that! Something's wrong.*

Karin turned toward the driver's seat to tell the mother superior to stop the car.

The nun was looking up, adjusting the visor. A red mark was visible on the bottom of her chin.

Karin froze.

She cast her mind back to the previous night's conversation with her siblings. She had seen a similarly placed bookmark very recently . . . on the arsonist.

At the same time, she realized what had been bothering her every time they described the assailant. *Shoes!*

The arsonist was wearing black shoes. Ren had described the man who had tried to kidnap China as "gray from head to toe." But then he corrected himself, remembering that the attacker had black hair. Surely he would have said if his shoes weren't gray, too?

China had described different clothes the other night. Karin hadn't allowed her to elaborate, worried that discussing the event would bring on another bout of panic. *Had she been referring to shoes as well?*

The man in the gray suit and the arsonist are two separate people after all!

They had assumed the arsonist was a man, but there was no reason it couldn't be a woman. *Or even a nun!*

Karin played out the scenario in her head. A nun could wear gray pants rolled up under her long skirts. When she lit the fire, she could just unroll them and hike her skirt beneath the parka to give the impression of a man. *The arsonist I saw yesterday, the person who came at me with the knife . . .*

Was right next to her.

Karin trembled. She had no idea what to do.

She couldn't speak. She slithered as close to the passenger door as possible, recoiling in fear. They were moving too fast to dive out of the car.

The mother superior curled her lips into a smile, but the rest of her face remained static. Her eyes remained impassive behind the reflective gleam of her spectacles. "What's wrong?"

Karin didn't count acting among her qualities.

The mother superior bared her teeth. "You've figured it out, haven't you? It doesn't matter now. I knew I was in trouble when China saw me. We live in the same convent! I would have inevitably done something to jog her memory. I had to put her to sleep."

The nun pulled a gun from somewhere inside her habit. She waved it casually to punctuate her speech, and continued driving with her other hand on the wheel. "It's all your fault, really. If you had been the only witness, I might have left her alone. I'm sure you recognize this little tool. My grandfather was in the army, and he left his weapon to my father. It's old, but well looked after. I imagine it still works beautifully. Shall we try it and see?"

Karin flattened further against the door and shook her head vigorously.

"Then behave yourself. You never know when a loaded gun might accidentally discharge."

They drove on in silence for a few moments. Suddenly, the car lurched to the left and sped toward a solid telephone pole. Karin shrieked and threw her arms across her face. Inertia flung her deep into her seat. The window handle dug into her side.

The telephone pole smashed off the side mirror and whipped past the car window. The mother superior had turned the wheel at the last second, returning the vehicle to the road.

Karin remained frozen in her seat.

"There," clucked the nun with the air of a schoolmarm. "Do you see? It would be so easy for an accident to happen. Passengers are far more likely to die in a car crash than the driver. It would behoove you not to think about grabbing the gun or any similar nonsense."

Karin could hear the threat, but was too petrified to answer. She was so terrified she didn't even allow herself to cry, although it's all she wanted to do. She didn't know what would set the mother superior off and didn't want to risk anything.

What's going to happen to us?

Karin knew China was drugged. *How long will it last? Where are we being taken? This maniac is never going to let us go. We know who she is!*

She stared out the window and pinched back tears.

What should I do? What should I do? Stop! Calm down!

Karin forced herself to breathe.

The sky was crimson outside the window, transforming the passing buildings into black silhouettes. The sun had almost complete set.

Karin's heart fluttered. Her family would be mobile soon. Anju had promised to send her bats to keep watch!

That's no good! Anju doesn't know where I am. She's gonna send her bats to the police station in Nishi-ku. They'll be useless there!

The changing landscape snapped her out of her reverie. Nothing looked familiar. *Where the hell are we going anyway?*

Karin knew she had to leave some sort of clue behind. Something that would lead her family to her. Or at least the bats.

She'd seen a movie once where a lost army squad had thrown out some colored balls that spat colored smoke for helicopters to home in on. But she didn't have anything that useful on her. She wouldn't be able to make oncoming traffic understand her predicament without the mother superior noticing.

She needed something that Anju would know belonged to her. Something the bats would see and report back on.

An old fairy tale sprang to mind.

"Sweat!" Karin blurted nervously. "It's hot. Is it okay if I use my hankie to wipe my face? I'm getting sweat in my eyes."

Karin was only half acting. The car had no air conditioning and seemed on the verge of boiling. She had sweat pooling on her brow and dripping from her black hair.

The mother superior glanced sideways at her. "Try anything funny and you'll regret it."

"I won't! I swear!" Karin shook her head violently.

She reached into her tote and found the paper bag full of cookies she had baked for China. Pretending to rummage for her handkerchief, she carefully tore the sticker holding the bag closed. She hid a stack of cookies in the handkerchief and withdrew the bundle.

Pretending to wipe sweat from her neck, Karin dropped a cookie out of the window onto to the road. A few seconds later, she dropped another. She was still pressed tight in the corner of her seat. She could drop cookies out the window with very little motion.

Karin had no idea if she was timing the cookie drops correctly or if she had enough cookies to lead all the way to wherever they were going. But it was better than nothing, and short of spitting out the window she had no way of leaving a trail.

Do bats even like cookies? But she couldn't think about that now. Anju *had* to find them somehow.

When the last of the cookies in her handkerchief fell to the pavement, Karin sunk her hand into the tote to fish out more. Her blood ran cold when the paper bag rustled.

"What are you doing?!" snapped the nun.

Karin froze, one hand in the bag. She stopped breathing and willed her heartbeat to follow suit.

"Um . . ." she wasn't sure what to do. Say she was having a snack? Fear clamped her throat shut and she found herself unable to speak.

The mother superior looked annoyed. "Give me your phone."

"Huh?"

"Don't play smart with me. You were going to message somebody, right? Hand it over."

Karin exhaled slowly. She frantically grabbed for her cell phone before the nun told her to hand over the entire bag. She finally found the handset and held it out.

The nun snatched the phone and tossed it over her shoulder into the back seat.

Karin shivered, but luck had been on her side.

She had overturned the cookie bag while rooting around for the phone, spilling cookies all over the inside of her tote. She could now pick them up without making any noise.

More importantly, the mother superior had let her guard down after taking the phone, convinced that Karin had no means of communication. She never noticed Karin's overdone sweat wiping.

Karin continued dropping cookies out the window, always glancing at the nun out of the corner of her eye to make sure she wasn't being watched. But eventually her luck ran out.

Karin reached into the back but couldn't find any more cookies. She had already dropped the last one. *No way! There must be something else I can throw out there.*

But she couldn't find anything suitable in her bag.

While Karin panicked, the mother superior yanked the wheel hard to the right. Karin slammed into the door and dropped her bag.

The car drove through an open iron gate and stopped in a concrete courtyard.

"Ow!" Karin rubbed her head as she looked out the window. They were parked next to a cement building that reminded her of school. A few of the darkened windows were broken. Weeds and other plants overran the facade. The building looked as if it had been abandoned for a long time.

The mother superior hopped out of the car and barked at Karin to do the same. "Bring your bag," she added. "Come over here and take China out of her seat. I just gave her some mild sleeping pills, so if she's too heavy to carry just slap her around until she wakes up."

Karin opened her door to the jangle of metal coins raining on the asphalt. Her wallet had come open when the tote fell on the floor. The car was parked on an incline, and several of the coins rolled down the hill toward the main street. "My wallet!" she wailed.

"Leave them!" snapped the nun. "They aren't important."

Karin looked up and saw the mother superior punctuating her point with the gun. She knew she had to do what she was told, even if it meant losing three dollars in change.

Karin wrestled with China, but the novice proved unwieldy. The nun sighed with exasperation.

"Wake up, China!" She still had the gun pointed at Karin's head.

China sprung out of the car like a jack-in-the-box. "Yes, ma'am!" She spoke automatically, but a moment later realized something wasn't right. "Uh. This isn't the police station. Mother Superior? What—?" China caught her breath when she saw the gun.

"The mother superior is the arsonist," Karin hissed.

China stared at her in shock. "No! How can you say that?!"

But she couldn't argue with the gun pointed at her new friend's head.

The mother superior jerked her head toward the concrete building. "Walk around me. The entrance is over there. It isn't locked."

"Mother Superior . . ." China whispered, grasping the situation at last. "Why are you doing this? How can you . . . ?"

Karin took China's hand and led her toward the door. "Do as she says, China."

The glass door was smashed into pieces, but Karin opened the frame anyway. The nun followed them, the gun in one hand and a black bag in the other.

Dust ground under their shoes. The linoleum floor was peeling almost as badly as the posters on the wall. Cheap veneer showed through fading paint on the walls. The building was completely abandoned, although its former use was immediately obvious.

"A hospital?" Karin whispered. Medical signs hung above various doors. The light of the setting sun through the broken windows revealed gurneys and medical equipment.

"It went bankrupt shortly after the dotcom bust," the mother superior lectured behind them. "An economy of greed shut the place down once the patients got priced out. We looked at this place last year when there was talk of moving the convent. It was too big for our purposes, of course, and we never did raise the money. But they never found a buyer . . . Now, head up those stairs."

Karin obeyed silently.

But China's sense of betrayal proved stronger than her fear. She spun to face her former mentor and let loose. "What the hell's the matter with you? All this time, you've guided me in my growth. Guided all the sisters. How can you be the arsonist? I don't understand!"

The mother superior didn't seem to mind the outburst. "Of course you don't understand. You think only of playing with boys and forget all about your prayers."

"I don't! I was . . ." China turned red.

The mother superior turned her attentions to Karin. "You, too. Far more concerned with staying out at night with boys than with a family that worries about you. You're the same as *that* woman."

Karin's ears pricked up at the sudden note of loathing and bile in the nun's voice. *Who is this other woman? What is she talking about?*

They reached the top of the stairs. The mother superior gestured toward the right with her gun. Their footsteps echoed in the windowless corridor. The sound reverberated and grew louder. Karin found it distressing.

The trio walked toward the end of the hallway and passed through a set of double doors, one of which was standing open. Urged silently onward, the girls went through them and entered a vast room.

The chamber had previously been used for physical therapy, but most of the usable equipment had already been carted away. Pulleys hung from the ceiling like wild vines. A set of parallel bars lurked in the corner. A scattering of mats left on the floor were slashed open, foam spilling out like guts.

There's no other way out. Both girls had the same thought simultaneously. They held hands in silent terror.

The gun poked Karin in the small of her back.

"Farther in," the mother superior ordered. "Sit down in front of those parallel bars. China, I want you to get the roll of tape that's sitting on that cardboard box over there and bind Karin's legs. When you're finished, do your own."

China wailed. "Please, stop this! How is this God's will?"

"Kiyomi was a good girl," the mother superior said abruptly. Her voice took on a fresh warmth that made her seem all the more frightening to Karin.

China took a step backward and bit her lip. She fought back tears as she grabbed the tape and walked over to Karin.

"I'm sorry," she whispered. China wrapped the tape around her friend's legs several times. It was thin but strong. Karin knew she wouldn't be able to wriggle free.

The mother superior carried on talking. "My younger sister's child. That stupid woman broke up with her lover and made a beeline straight for my place. She dumped Kiyomi on my lap. A four-year-old child! Can you believe it? But Kiyomi was such a good girl. So well behaved. So smart. She always listened. I could hardly believe she was really that idiot's daughter. She was an angel."

Her tone veered wildly depending on whether she was talking about her sister or her niece. Her mania did nothing to soothe Karin and China.

"I was angered by the extra work at first. But I was making more than enough money to care for a child, and the child welfare center would have been a nightmare of paperwork. So I took her in. I realized what a good girl she was once we started living together. She watched TV quietly until I got home, and then greeted me properly. 'Welcome home, Aunt Kyoko'!" The mother superior took on a warped tone as she imitated the young girl.

Karin blanched. Didn't serial killers always get rid of their victims once they learned the kidnapper's name? At least, that's what happened in the movies.

The mother superior still had the gun trained on the girls, but she was lost in thought. Her voice was incongruously filled with love. "My sister met a new man a year later and announced she was taking Kiyomi with her to America. The courts decided it would be better for Kiyomi to live with her birth mother and a new stepfather than her spinster aunt. So I had to let her go. A lot happened since then. I quit my job and entered the convent. My sister never called, never wrote. But I knew Kiyomi was a good girl, so I was sure she was well loved and happy." A self-deprecating edge crept into her voice.

Karin silently put her hands behind her, afraid to speak. China taped her friend's wrists and then set about binding her own legs.

The mother superior came over and checked to make sure the bindings were tight. Then she taped China's hands behind her back. Neither girl could move, but the mother superior wanted better insurance.

"Ow!" Karin yelped. The mother superior had grabbed her shoulder and yanked backward, pressing Karin against one of the vertical poles supporting the parallel bars. The nun unwound a length of tape and bound Karin to the pole by her neck.

"What are you doing?!"

"If you struggle, the tape will strangle you." The nun taped China to the neighboring pole.

Karin choked back tears. Grimy windows revealed that the sun had set completely. *Anju! Send your bats to find me! Please!*

Karin knew she had to buy some time. She called out to the mother superior calmly, so as not to set her off. "Wait! Don't stop in the middle of the story. I want to know the rest. What happened to Kiyomi?"

The answer was simple.

"She died."

Karin bit her lip. She had half-expected this to be the case.

China jerked her head in surprise and choked herself on the tape. She grunted and coughed.

"I only found out recently," the nun said. "But she died in a car accident eight years ago. She was trapped in the car and burned to death. She was taken to America, only to die." She no longer spoke in the gentle tone she had previously used to talk about Kiyomi. Her voice was flat and cold, devoid of emotion. The mother superior went out into the hall, leaving the door open behind her.

Her footsteps faded away.

Karin and China exchanged glances.

"Where is she going?" Karin wondered aloud.

"I don't know. Is she . . . Is she the arsonist we saw yesterday?"

Karin explained what she had discovered. China deflated.

"She was out last Friday," China whispered. "And two days ago. And yesterday. She was away from the convent every time a fire broke out. She's been very strange ever since the first fires. Always lost in thought."

Karin remembered the mother superior's tone when she said Kiyomi had burned to death. "That might have been when she found out this Kiyomi girl was dead," she reasoned.

The nun appeared to have really loved her niece. She must have consoled herself with the thought that Kiyomi was safe and well while in America. When news at last arrived, it was to inform her of the child's violent death eight years ago.

The mother superior had been oddly critical of "family" and "playing with boys" in the car. Karin wondered if her love for Kiyomi had twisted into a pathological hatred of youth. But she knew this was no time for discerning motive. The important thing was to try to get away before the nun returned.

The only thing binding Karin and China to the parallel bars was the tape at their necks. But that was the problem. If they strained against the tape, they might strangle themselves. Their hands were taped behind their backs, preventing them from ripping free.

Karin struggled for a few moments anyway, coughing as she strained against her bonds. Finally she gave up. "China, do you know anyone who might come save us?"

"No. Everyone in the convent knows I went out with Mother Superior today. All she has to do is tell everyone I transferred to a different convent for safety reasons. All of the sisters would believe her."

"Maybe my—" Karin brought herself up short. She could hear the footsteps growing louder, accompanied by the sound of something dragging on the concrete floor.

The mother superior had a penlight in one hand and was dragging a mattress with the other. She hauled the mattress over to a pile of mats at the edge of the rehabilitation room. She topped off the heap with cardboard boxes, torn curtains, and Karin's abandoned tote bag.

Karin gasped.

The mother superior took something out of her own bag. In the dim light, it appeared to be a plastic bottle. But as soon as she removed the cap, Karin smelled kerosene.

"Wait!" she shrieked. "You can't!"

Karin could hear liquid spilling onto the pile. After a moment, the bottle was empty. The mother superior tossed it on top of the pile and pulled another object out of her pocket. There was a flimsy scraping sound, and a small flame appeared.

The match illuminated the nun's features as it flared to life. She smiled inhumanly. "Let the flames cleanse you."

She flicked the match on to the pile of cardboard and rags. A second later the mound exploded into a blazing pyre.

China screamed.

The fire had taken hold on the makeshift pyre and now began inching outward. Karin knew it was only a matter of time until the flames reached the walls and ceiling.

The mother superior wandered out of the room again. Karin could hear her footsteps fade away as she descended the stairwell at the end of the corridor.

China was panicking, completely lost in her own reality. Her face was white as a sheet, illuminated by the flames. She flailed around awkwardly, trying in vain to get away from the fire no matter how badly the tape dug into her throat. "No! Stop! Somebody save me!"

"China! Calm down!" Karin was terrified. But her friend's panic triggered something cold and controlled inside her. Any chance at survival would be lost if they both panicked.

"No! Mommy! Help! I'm scared!"

Karin gave up trying to comfort China. She tried to dig into the tape around her wrists with her fingernails.

Fortunately, the mattress had been lying in a damp room. It had flared up where the mother superior had scattered kerosene, but seemed reluctant to spread beyond that. A cloud of white steam rose where flames might have been. But Karin knew the fire would grow bigger as the heat dried out the mattress.

I've got to get this tape off!

Karin desperately worked her fingers, but the tape was too sticky. The more she struggled, the tighter the tape got on her neck. She wasn't sobbing like China, but she was scared enough for tears to stream down her cheeks.

China had taped her legs together a little too tightly. The bindings had clamped off her circulation and Karin could feel her blood vessels throbbing. She was so frightened she felt nauseous. The fire made her hot all over, and her canines were lengthening into fangs—

Huh?

A terrible thought struck her. Karin ran her tongue over her teeth to be certain. How could fire make her canines grow?

No way! You've got to be kidding me!

Karin banged her feet against the door in a panic.

It's here!

Her pulse was up, her body felt hot, she could barely breathe, she felt nauseous . . . All symptoms of her blood rush.

This can't be happening! I just bit someone two days ago!

She reckoned it was down to China and the mother superior. The nun's psychosis was deeply rooted in unhappiness over the death of her niece. As for China . . .

"No! Fire is so scary! I hate it! Daddy! Mommy!"

China was in a blind panic brought about by the intense fear of fires her unhappy childhood experience had given her. She was beside herself with terror.

The two women had enough unhappiness between them to trigger Karin's vampiric instincts and set off an abnormally powerful blood rush. *And at a time like this!*

Karin was unnerved by the prospect. *If I start spouting blood now, I'll lose too much and get anemic! Then I won't be able to move!*

This was not a situation where she could afford to pass out from a torrential nosebleed.

"Agh!" The reaction she had been holding back all this time came at last; an emotional dam burst that resulted in a cascade of wails and tears.

"Anju! Come save me! I don't wanna die! Somebody help me!"

Her voice was so loud the glass shook in the windows behind her. Her bound hands trashed around and her feet floundered uselessly. She coughed fitfully as the tape dug into her throat but she paid no attention.

"I don't wanna die! Please!"

And then she heard a slight tearing sound from the tape around her wrists.

It's breaking!

The tape was weakened. She grasped desperately to this faint hope. If the tape had a cut somewhere, she could follow the fold and tear it all the way through. Once her hands were free, she would be able to free her throat as well.

Karin threw all of her strength into her left wrist and twisted as far as possible. The tape dug into her arms. She could scarcely breathe. Her body was so hot. The blood rush made her body temperature rise steadily.

Her pulse was so strong, her heart felt like it was going to burst.

She knew she had to find a way to break the tape before the blood rush went passed the tipping point and left her unconscious. She was terrified of burning alive.

"Break! Break!" But her pleas were lost in the roar of the fire.

The flames moved from the mattress to the wall.

 **CHIBI VAMPIRE AND THE SAVIOR**

Man, I'm out." The truck driver sighed mournfully as he shook an empty carton of Mild Sevens. He glanced hopefully at the boy sitting next to him and moved his foot off the gas.

"Hey, Usui. There's a gas station at the next light. I'm gonna pull off and pick up some cigarettes."

The truck eased to a stop at the side of the road. The driver tossed a five hundred yen coin to Kenta. "There's a vending machine by the bathroom. Grab me a pack of Mild Sevens, will ya? And a cold coffee, no sugar. You can buy yourself something with the change."

"Sure! Thanks!" Kenta hopped out of the truck and ran over to the vending machine. The sun had set, but it was still hot. He dropped some coins into the adjacent machine and punched the button for a cold soft drink. The can popped out of the dispenser. He took a swig and then held the frosty can up to his sweaty forehead.

It wasn't until he bent down to retrieve the change from the vending machine that he saw the cookie.

He picked it up uncertainly. *Maybe it'll still be edible if I dust it off,* he reasoned. *Oh! There's another one!*

Kenta had an eagle eye when it came to food. There was a second cookie on the ground about thirty feet down the road. And another beyond that, a cookie that had been crushed underfoot but still bore the telltale color of yummy delight.

What a tragic waste!

Kenta wanted to follow the trail and see how many cookies he could collect. But he could hardly ask Sakada to pull over every time he spied another one. The driver would get annoyed.

A little piece of Kenta died at the thought of cookies gone to waste.

What kind of person throws food away like this? These look homemade. Baked to such a lovely shade of brown and decorated with dried fruit. Karin makes cookies just like these . . .

Kenta stood bolt upright. These *were* the cookies Karin gave him. The color, shape, and toppings were exactly the same.

But his share was safely in his bag, stashed away for an emergency. He'd only eaten a few since leaving Julian. There was no way he could have dropped them here.

Karin said she'd made some for China, too. Did she throw these away? I don't think nuns would waste food. I can't see China throwing away something Karin made by hand. They'd be in a garbage can somewhere anyway, not spaced out like this.

Kenta knew that one of the girls had to have dropped the cookies. But neither of them was supposed to be in Sanjo-shi. One thing was abundantly clear; the cookies were spaced evenly on the ground. It was like something out of Hansel and Gretel.

Did something happen to them?

Kenta started to worry.

Sakada honked at him, having grown sick of watching Kenta stand by the side of the road, scratching his head.

Kenta dashed over and gave the driver the requested cigarettes and coffee. "I'm sorry, Sakada. I just remembered something important. Is it okay if I take off now?"

"What?"

"It's important! Please!"

"Uh . . ."

Now it was the driver's turn to scratch his head. "I guess so. Go ahead. But isn't your bag back at the office?"

"I've got it right here." Kenta hoisted the bag over his shoulder as proof.

Sakada waived and the truck drove off with a hiss of hydraulics.

Kenta wondered if he had made the right decision. He didn't even know which cookie was dropped first—a key indicator of which direction to start walking. If it really *was* a trail, it would only get harder to spy each new cookie in the deepening twilight.

Kenta picked up another cookie and dropped it into his bag. Sometimes they were quite close together; others were a hundred feet or more apart. He had to pick a direction at random at intersections, doubling back if no cookies presented themselves.

The trail finally grew cold on a back road. There was scant lighting away from the main strip, and Kenta knew he was going to have problems finding something as small as a cookie.

Suddenly, a black sedan tore out of a gap between two concrete walls, screeching into a perpendicular turn to shoot off down the road. There were no other cars on the road. No sign of anything to create such a rush.

The car vanished over the horizon, leaving Kenta alone with his thoughts.

What do these cookies really mean? Did I read too much into them?

He half expected to hear a gunshot or find himself before a creepy old house. Yet there was nothing but empty road and concrete walls. Kenta started to doubt himself. He'd been so caught up in following the trail of cookies that he hadn't been paying attention to the streets.

He was lost.

Something glittered on the road ahead of him.

Lucky! Kenta ran over to the glint and discovered a one-yen coin.

Another gleamed by the side of the road, next to a pair of iron gates. He had just seen the black car come through them. He looked around tentatively, but the car was nowhere to be seen.

He didn't know whether taking the coins was right or wrong, but greed got the better of him. He pocketed the coin and looked through the gates. A ten-yen coin lay on the asphalt up ahead.

Kenta noticed the iron gates were covered with rust. The garden beyond was overrun with weeds, and the building in the courtyard looked abandoned. Kenta went in without a second thought.

He picked up ten yen, then fifty. Eventually he had collected nearly four hundred yen. But the tally soon grew too high to be a happy coincidence.

Why is so much money scattered around here?

He considered his surroundings once more, finally focusing on the ruined building. His ears perked up at the faint sound of screams emanating from within.

Suddenly, Kenta remembered why he had come here. It wasn't for cookies or coins. He was worried something had happened to Karin and China.

The screams continued.

That's a girl's voice! It couldn't be Karin, could it?

Kenta knew it didn't matter whose voice it was. He had to check. He made his way over to the building, aided by the feeble light of the streetlights on the other side of the wall.

What was that?

Kenta froze as he reached the door. He thought he heard something scrabbling over the wall. He stepped back and peered into the darkness.

"Is somebody there?"

There was no answer. The screams continued inside. Was it his imagination? Or had someone walked past the wall? Kenta returned to the door and opened it wide.

The screams were instantly louder.

"No! Fire! I'm so scared! Save me!"

"Gah! Why won't you break?!"

He knew both voices . . . and the unmistakable crackle and roar of fire. Any lingering doubts vanished. *Karin and China! The arsonist must have found them!*

Kenta took the stairs three at a time. His long legs were useful in moments like these—not that he made a habit of dashing into burning buildings.

The screams suddenly cut off when he reached the third floor. A chill ran down his spine and Kenta stopped breathing. He didn't dare speculate.

I'm not gonna let anything happen to them!

He charged down the hall. The screams had lasted long enough for Kenta to know where he was going. He could hear the fire raging through the open door at the end of the hallway and he could see the orange lick of flames.

Please be okay!

Kenta burst through the doors. A wall of heat immediately smacked him in the face.

"Karin! China!" he called, looking around. His knees buckled when he saw the girls.

China was leaning against the parallel bars. Her cheeks were flushed red and her habit's veil was missing. Her bare throat was exposed.

Karin was on her knees next to China, both arms wrapped tightly around her. Her eyes were moist, and her lips were pressed against the novice's throat.

China's body trembled with each flicked of Karin's mouth.

Delicate moans escaped her lightly parted lips. Anyone unaware of Karin's true nature would have taken the scene for a lover's embrace.

Kenta did a double take. "What the hell are you *doing?*"

"Eep!" Karin spun around, terrified. Her long fangs gleamed in her mouth, a few red drops lingering at their tips.

"Kenta? What are you doing here?"

"Shut up!" Kenta knew what Karin was. He knew she had bit China to inject her excess blood into the novice. But still, Kenta couldn't contain himself. "What on Earth do you think you're doing? Do you see the fire burning on the other side of the room? Is this really the time?"

He didn't tell her how his blood ran cold at the thought of her dying when she stopped screaming. He had feared the worst.

China's body slipped out of Karin's hands. She sprawled out on the floor, unconscious from the shock of being bitten.

"But . . ." Karin flailed her arms around. She tried to defend herself. "There wasn't time to make a break for it! I would have overflowed! I managed to frcc China and me but that was the limit. If I got a nosebleed, I would have passed out and we'd both be dead now! It's embarrassing, but I had no choice!"

Kenta noticed the scraps of tape on the girls' wrists and ankles. They weren't here by accident. "Fine. We can talk about it later. We've got to get out of here!"

The fire had already reached the wall. Acrid black smoke filled the room. Kenta had heard that some paints and wallpaper glue emitted poisonous fumes when burned. They had to get out of the building before they were overcome.

Kenta bent over China and shook her awake.

"Karin? Am I still dreaming?"

"China, snap out of it!"

Karin leaned in frantically. "We have to run! There's still time!"

China bolted upright. Her expression froze as her eyes settled on Karin.

"Those fangs! Karin?" China shoved Kenta aside and scooted backward across the floor, trying to put distance between herself and the others. "It wasn't a dream! Those fangs . . . You really did bite me!"

Karin covered her mouth with both hands, but it was too late.

China shook her head in horror. She touched her neck and brought her hands away covered in blood. Her expression grew taught with fear.

"Karin! What did you do to me? Did you *bite* me? In the neck? It hurts! What did you do? Those fangs! You have fangs! Did you drink my blood?"

Karin shook her head violently. "No! I didn't drink any blood!"

"Liar! Why else would you bite me? Why do I have these holes in my neck? You're a vampire! An unholy beast!"

Karin's denials had strengthened China's resolve. She scrambled about wildly, oblivious to the fire. "Get away from me! Vampire! You're trying to make me one of you!"

Karin had no answer to that.

China edged farther away. She pulled a rosary out of her pocket and waived the cross in front of her. Her petite hands were shaking, her voice filled with the fear all humans instinctively have in the presence of the undead. The room was sweltering with the heat of the fire, but all color had drained from her face. China had tears in her eyes.

Karin had no reaction to the cross. But she was visibly shaken by China's words.

"I don't want to be a creature of the night. A monster! How could you do this to me? This is demonic!"

Kenta knew Karin well enough to understand the signs she was broadcasting. In a few moments, she would collapse onto the ground in a heap of sobs and snot, crying so hard she would barely be able to breathe. Whatever had happened, there wasn't time for that now. He had to interfere.

"Stop!" Kenta stepped between the two girls. He looked directly into China's eyes, blocking Karin from view.

"Karin did bite you. But you don't feel any different now, do you?"

"Kenta?"

"Just because she bit you doesn't mean she drank your blood. She didn't do anything bad to you. Trust me. There's no reason to attack her like that. Please stop."

Kenta could hear Karin's throat tightening behind him as she choked back sobs.

China peered anxiously at Kenta's mouth. "You're not a vampire, are you?"

"Nope. I'm just a regular guy. Karin is just a little different. But that's no reason for turning against her like this. It's just cruel!" He couldn't bear people who ostracized others or behaved without mercy. He would never let himself become like that, and had little time for those who would treat his friends in that way.

"What did Karin really do to you?" he continued. "Sure, she bit you. But she tried to save you from the fire. And she helped you yesterday, too! How can you call her a monster? You're worse than she could ever be!"

China didn't answer. She shifted her gaze between Kenta and Karin in confusion. Her expression finally settled into one of shame.

"You're right," she admitted. "I've said such terrible things. I'm really sorry."

"Forget it." Karin waved a hand nonchalantly. "I did bite you. Anyone would be surprised. Besides, I think we probably have bigger problems."

The trio was suddenly aware of standing in the center of a blazing inferno.

"Run!"

All three ran for the door. But it was too late.

"Enough of that."

A quiet voice echoed from the hall. The tone was so cold they stopped in their tracks.

A figure appeared in the open doorway. The mother superior stood before them impassively, her glasses glinting with the reflected light of the fire. She had the penlight in one hand and a gun in the other.

"What?" Kenta wasn't on the same page of the others.

"I parked around the corner waiting for the fire to catch. I thought I saw someone come in and came back to check. And a good thing I did, too."

Kenta took in the expression on the girls' faces and solved the riddle. "The man in gray was just some random attacker. You're the arsonist!"

Karin nodded jerkily.

The mother superior looked at the three of them, then at the fire. "Go back. Now!"

"Don't be stupid! We'll burn to death!" Kenta shouted.

The nun's expression grew even colder. "Exactly," she said smoothly. "The fire will cleanse you."

The penlight was redundant with the flames so bright, so she put it in her pocket and gripped the gun with both hands. The nun took a step forward.

"Mother Superior," China whispered, her voice trembling. "I . . ." Suddenly, China spun around and ran directly toward the fire.

Karin yelped with surprise. "China! What are you doing?"

Kenta remembered what Karin had told him. The very sight of fire was enough to send China into a blind panic. And yet here she was running toward the fire. Something wasn't right.

The move even stunned the mother superior. They were on the third floor, so China couldn't jump out a window. And the armed nun stood by the only door.

But China wasn't bolting blindly into the darkness.

She ran to the wall directly behind the burning mattress. She swept down and grabbed a red cylinder in both hands, heaving it into the air.

Kenta's eyes widened when he realized what China had picked up. It was covered in dust and almost gray, and there was no telling if it even worked anymore, but it was clearly a fire extinguisher.

China popped out the safety pin and aimed the short hose at the fire.

"China!" The mother superior barked, but China had already squeezed the hand and unleashed a torrent of white foam.

The recoil knocked China back a few paces, but she gritted her teeth and pressed on. White bubbles collided with yellow flames, choking off the fire's oxygen supply and stamping out its burning tendrils. China extinguished the blaze in just a few seconds, although time stood still for Karin and Kenta.

The room plunged into darkness once more when the last snatch of fire fell before the onslaught. Nobody moved. Hissing cinders in the foam marred the stunned silence.

"China . . . You weren't scared of the fire. How could that be?" The mother superior moaned.

China turned to face her former mentor, the heavy fire extinguisher still in her hands. Even in the dim light, the other three could see her eyebrows knotted in a determined scowl.

"I don't know," she said quietly. "But I always wanted to be like this. To conquer the flames instead of cowering before them. I longed to do that."

Kenta realized with a start that China was now under the influence of Karin's blood. Her plasma changed her victims psychologically as a bizarre side effect. Apathetic people would suddenly become passionate. Arrogant people would become humble. Anxious people would become confident and relaxed. Perhaps her vampiric blood allowed people to become who they had always wanted to be.

China had been terrified of fire. But the new blood pulsing inside her had freed her from her phobia. It explained why she had become so impassioned with Karin rather than fleeing the fire moments earlier.

Kenta felt himself begin to relax with the danger of burning to death now gone.

But the mother superior still held a weapon.

"Novice!" she snarled. There was a sharp crack from her hands and the floor between Kenta and Karin exploded into chunks of concrete.

The two friends leapt backward in surprise.

China froze in place, the extinguisher clanging to the floor beside her.

The smell of gunpowder drifted through the newly silent hallway.

Kenta felt a faint glimmer of hope break through his fear. *She had been aiming at China, but hit the ground a dozen feet away. She's a terrible shot!*

But he knew her lack of skill was a double-edged sword. There was no way to predict where bullets might strike. They couldn't make any careless moves. A wrong step could cause the mother superior to squeeze off another round. Without a clear aim, the bullets might hit anybody.

Karin and China remained perfectly still. Kenta knew they were thinking the same thing.

The nun's hands moved very slowly. Her face twisted into an expression of unvarnished loathing. She took in each of them in turn.

"Absolutely unforgivable," she said. Her voice echoed around the darkened hallway.

Kenta panicked. *Do I take a chance and lunge at her? What if she shot somebody?*

The dull gleam of the barrel finally settled on someone.

"*Me?*" Karin screamed in surprise. She was the closest to the mother superior. The two were just a few feet apart. The nun seemed to be a terrible shot, but Karin had no doubt that they were too close for that to matter much.

"Not me!" Karin cried. "I don't wanna be shot!"

The mother superior arched an eyebrow. She opened her mouth, but somebody else spoke before she could spit out an epitaph.

"Shut up, Karin." A deep voice snarled from deeper in the hallway.

"What?" The nun began to turn around, but a hand emerged from the darkness and clamped around her wrist. It squeezed with incredible force. Her face twisted in pain and she dropped the gun.

A stoic young man with platinum blond hair stood behind her. Nobody had heard him approach.

"Ren!" Karin rushed over to her brother.

"Why is he here?" gasped China. Her cheeks flashed bright red.

"China?" Kenta and Karin questioned simultaneously.

"Nothing!" China backpedaled anxiously, denying the question implicit in their gaze.

The source of the surprise barely glanced at his sister and her friends. Instead, Ren kept focused on the mother superior.

Kenta shuddered. There as something lurking in that steely gaze he hadn't seen before. Ren's eyes were generally a dim red. But now they gleamed with gold. His pupils narrowed into vertical slits, like those of a cat. Kenta shivered instinctively.

Whatever Kenta was feeling, the mother superior was even more terrified. She struggled uselessly in his iron grip. "Let me go!"

"A woman," he murmured. "A little past her prime, but nothing insurmountable. Starting all those fires made you plenty stressed."

Kenta gulped. He could see two fangs glittering in Ren's mouth.

China let out a little shriek.

"Ren! You can't!" Karin yelled, but Ren ignored her. His golden gaze rested on the mother superior's throat.

"It's a shame I can only do this once," he said, reaching out for her neck. Long, nimble fingers pulled her collar back, and a moment later he bit into her throat from behind.

Karin and her friends were frozen with horrible fascination. The only sound in the room was a liquid, slurping noise.

It went on.

And on.

And still on.

They had been paralyzed with shock and fear, but the effect gradually wore off as Ren's feast continued.

Kenta and China both looked inquiringly at Karin.

"Karin . . ."

"He's your brother . . ."

Karin cast her gaze feebly at the ground. "I know."

Ren still had his arm tightly around the psychotic nun. His feeding looked more like the passionate embrace of two lovers, just as Karin and China had appeared when Kenta broke into the rehabilitation room.

Kenta rubbed his forehead. He definitely had a headache coming on.

China shifted her gaze from Ren to Karin. She was far too embarrassed to look at Ren for long.

Karin, for her part, was still staring at the ground.

"What will happen to the mother superior?" China asked.

"Um. She'll have a lot less stress," Karin said. "But after that, I don't really know. My brother is the enemy of women."

"But the mother superior is a *nun!*"

"Ren doesn't really discriminate based on occupation. Anyway, don't talk to me! I'm totally mortified that my brother is the worst womanizer in the history of time! Argh!" Karin cast her gaze around for a hole into which she could crawl.

Somebody smacked her on the head.

"That's the thanks I get for saving you? Ungrateful little witch," Ren spat. He had finished feeding while the others averted their gaze. The nun lay on the ground, immobile. She had lost a lot of blood, or maybe had been incapacitated by other means.

"Already finished?" Karin sang.

"Drained her. Wiped her memories. I'd have preferred to take some time and savor her, but she's gonna be in police custody for a while." Ren looked at China. Her wimple had fallen off when Karin bit her, and the collar of her habit was pulled down. The two pinpricks on her throat were clearly visible.

"Karin, you bit her?"

"Um. Yeah. The blood rush . . ."

"Okay." Ren nodded and strode over to China.

The novice stepped backward in surprise. Ren reached out and put a hand to her face. Her body stiffened, then crumpled to the floor.

"China!" Kenta called.

"What did you do?!" Karin screamed. The two friends darted toward China.

Ren turned around. The gold light had left his eyes and his fangs had reverted to ordinary human canines. But his face betrayed his anger.

Karin and Kenta stopped, intimidated.

"I erased her memories, of course!" Ren barked. "We're not letting anyone else know about you! Come on, Karin. We're going home!"

"Just like that?"

"Retard!" Ren thumped Karin on the head again.

"Ow! Why do you always hit me?"

"We can't stick around for the clean up," Ren said, annoyed. "I had to give up the hunt to come all the way out here just to save you. You should be grateful there was a stressed woman here for me to feed on."

"You didn't come here to drink?"

"Why would I be all the way out here in the middle of nowhere? Anju sent a bat my way and asked me to rescue you. She could have sent her bats to observe, but that wouldn't have helped you. I was the closest one."

"So Anju was watching after all," Karin said to herself.

"I keep telling you to stop making trouble for your sister. You'd better thank her when we get back."

"I will. And thank you, too."

"I erased the last thirty minutes' of memories for both sisters. We can't have the cops taking you in for questioning. There's no telling what might tip them off to your true nature. We'd better get out of here before anyone else gets here. Let him handle the rest." Ren indicated Kenta with a disinterested wave.

Kenta pointed at himself in surprise. "Me?"

"Of course." Ren glowered. "I told you I don't trust you. I'm only letting you keep your memories because Anju asked me to. You didn't see Karin here. At all. Got it?"

The hallway grew darker as he spoke; the streetlights outside dimmed ominously. Kenta looked outside a window and saw countless black shapes flapping through the sky.

Bats!

Enough bats to block the light.

These were clearly not ordinary bats. They were servants of the vampires. When Kenta had first found out the truth about Karin, Ren had showed up to threaten him. The vampire had been surrounded by a flock of bats blotting out the sky. The next day, Karin's parents had later abducted him to prove their point.

"If you so much as hint about my sister's involvement . . ." Ren began. "I don't have to explain what will happen, do I?"

Kenta shuddered.

"Ren! Kenta hasn't done anything!" Karin whined.

"Shut up," Ren snapped.

The words cowed Karin into silence.

A bat swooped through a broken windowpane and flapped around Ren. It appeared to be communicating with him. After a moment, Ren grabbed his sister with alarm. "The fire department is on its way here!"

"Huh?"

"A passerby must have seen the fire through the windows and called it in. The trucks are on their way. We need to get out of here. Tell your friend not to screw this up."

Ren dragged Karin out the door and down the hall. The bats that had kept watch outside the window flew away.

"Sorry, Kenta!" Karin called out. But she was soon drowned out by the sound of approaching sirens.

Kenta would have preferred to flee like Karin and Ren. But the two nuns were lying unconscious on the floor, and someone had to explain to the authorities who the mother superior really was so that she wouldn't continue to be a threat.

"Oh, well." He decided to tell the firemen that he had been walking past the building and heard screams.

Multiple sets of sirens were outside the walls now.

One week later . . .

The weather grew hotter as the weeks gave way to August.

The trees around Julian were lush and green, filtering out much of the sunlight. The sounds of summer were deafening. The chorus of cicadas flooded into the restaurant as the backdoor swung open; it fell silent as soon as the door slammed shut.

Kenta entered the restaurant, coated in sweat. "Sorry I'm late!" he said when he noticed Karin in the hallway.

He dove into the men's locker room. Between the restaurant and the moving company and assorted odd jobs in between, he had little time for socializing.

"Hurry up. The coffee crowd is going to start pouring in here any minute now," Karin said. She grabbed a box of disposable chopsticks from the storeroom and swept into the main dining room.

Kenta found it hard to believe it had only been a week since they had been trapped in the abandoned hospital.

The mother superior had been arrested for arson. The case had been in the news every day, with the media abuzz over the idea of a murdering nun. Reporters spent hours of airtime going over her history and motives. But they never seemed to discuss the mysterious bite marks that had appeared on her and China's necks.

China . . . Neither Kenta nor Karin knew what had happened to her. The police were withholding details on China and Kenta on account of them both being minors. That made tracking her down difficult. The phones at the Saint Christina Convent were never answered these days—the mother superior's arrest probably had them ringing off the hook.

"Maaka, are you finished with that? Put it over there and clear table five. Hurry!" The manager directed the staff with both hands, generally getting in the way.

"Welcome to Julian!" Karin beamed as a new guest entered the restaurant.

There was no time to get lost in thought. Customer after customer flowed into Julian, hoping to take refuge from the heat in the air-conditioned dining room.

"Will that be all?"

"Here you go. Pudding parfait and an iced coffee."

"Are you ready to order?"

"That comes to one thousand and twenty yen."

They ran their feet off for two hours, and the sunlight grew red as dusk approached. Eventually the rush died down, giving Karin and Kenta the chance to chat as they cleared tables.

The front doors chimed to announce a customer. The two friends turned to welcome the newcomer, but stopped short.

A girl in a white habit stood in the doorway.

"Hello again, Karin, Kenta." China bowed. The collar of her habit covered the lingering remains of the bite mark on her throat.

Ren had erased her memories of the fire—and of Karin biting her. China had the same pleasant, tentative manner as before.

"I came to say goodbye."

A few minutes later, the three of them stood by the back entrance. The storeroom was sparse and utilitarian, but it had air conditioning and was therefore a good place to hang out.

China explained that she had no time to eat, and not enough money to order anything anyway. But she wanted to say goodbye to Karin and Kenta in person.

"Well, I'm glad you're safe," Karin said, relieved. "I was so worried the police would be mean to you. Maybe they thought you were cooperating with the mother superior or something when they found you both in the hospital."

China opened her eyes wide. "How do you know about the hospital? They didn't release my name to the press."

"I told her," Kenta said, swooping in to the rescue.

"Oh yes, Kenta was there," China said to herself. "I don't remember anything that happened at the hospital. But from what the police told me, it sounds like I was saved because he happened to be walking by. Thank you again."

"I heard screams and ran inside. You and the mother superior were already on the ground. Anybody would do what I did."

The mother superior hadn't been able to remember anything after drugging China in the car; her memories stopped before she picked up Karin at the restaurant. She instantly confessed to the arson cases.

One thing still bothered Karin. "What about the man in gray? He tried to kidnap you twice. I guess we were reading too much into it. He had nothing to do with anything?"

"Apparently he was arrested earlier this week," China said. She had given the police a full description of the man while being questioned about the fires. One of the detectives had immediately produced a photograph that matched her assailant. He had been picked up the same day for trying to snatch a junior high school girl.

"I wasn't the only one he was after," China continued. "Any time he saw a girl he liked, he would attack her. The police told me to file a report."

Kenta sighed. "What a creep. Nothing to do with the fires, then. Just some random pervert who coincidentally happened to attack you around the same time the blazes were started. There seem to be a lot of people like that these days. At least he's been arrested. You won't be attacked again. And with the arsonist arrested, too . . ."

"Everything is over," China agreed. "But I still don't understand how the mother superior could do what she did."

"The news said it was the shock of finding out her niece was dead," Karin explained. The media had picked up on her motives, exactly the same as China and Karin had surmised at the hospital. The nun had already had a fascination with fire, and hearing about her niece burning to death had pushed her over the edge. She became determined to cleanse everything with flames to clear their paths to heaven.

"Not her motive," China corrected. "I don't understand how the mother superior could have forgotten Jesus' teachings. She heard the sad news about her niece two months ago. But even after that, she was the same kind mentor she had always been. She still did good works, still prayed. The news makes her out to be evil incarnate, but she wasn't. I think something broke inside her heart."

"You aren't mad at her?" Karin wrinkled her nose in puzzlement.

"No. I wish I could talk with her, but they won't let me. If the new convent allows me, I would like to write her."

"The new convent? What do you mean?"

China explained that the mother superior had been the lynchpin holding the convent together. It wasn't just shock; none of the other sisters had been involved in finances or planning. The bishop decided to replace the entire staff and reform the convent altogether. All of the nuns were being transferred to a new location to help quiet the media buzz and try to restore some semblance of normality to the Saint Christina Convent.

"So where are you going?" Kenta asked.

China named an island in the Inland Sea.

"But that's so far!"

"Do they even *have* convents in a place like that?"

China smiled. "I've never lived near the ocean. I'm kind of looking forward to it. I leave the day after tomorrow. So I'm saying goodbye to everyone I know. Thank you both for everything." She winked cheekily. "And best of luck to the two of you."

"W-wait!" Kenta spluttered.

"You've got the wrong end of the stick!" Karin protested, her face bright red.

But China ignored them both. "I do have one vague memory. Like something out of a dream. I didn't tell the police about it, because it didn't have much to do with the case. But I remember you being there at the hospital, Karin."

The novice carefully studied their faces.

Karin was shocked. Select humans were capable of resisting vampire memory wipes. Was China one of these? But she could never acknowledge the possibility out loud.

Karin shook her head. "You're mistaken . . ."

China ignored the denials. "Karin was about to cry, because I'd said something cruel to her. I can't remember what that was. I don't know why I would say anything like that. But Kenta stepped in to defend you."

Karin's heart skipped a beat. Her body shook. China might have forgotten about the bite, but the trace of a few events after that lingered on.

"He said you weren't doing anything bad," China recalled thoughtfully. "He said I shouldn't try to make you feel bad. He was so mad at me. He said I was a worse person than you are. I could really feel the bond between you two. I was so ashamed after he scolded me . . ."

Kenta held his hands to his head and moaned quietly.

Karin knew how he felt. Most things said in the heat of the moment were embarrassing afterward, no matter how true they were. But they had to back out of this conversation quickly.

"That's quite a dream! I wasn't there. I was at home!"

"Yes, I know it's just a dream," China agreed. "But it was a good dream. It taught me something important. I'm still so inexperienced. I deserved that scolding. It guided me to a better way of thinking. I'm sure no one besides the Karin and Kenta in my dreams would have taught me this lesson as well. That's why I value it so much."

Karin couldn't tell if China actually believed it was a dream or was simply agreeing to keep the charade going. She smiled sweetly as the novice studied her hands.

"I have to go now," China said. "Thank you for everything."

"No, thank *you* for fixing my umbrella . . . and everything," Kenta offered.

"Take care, China," Karin said.

The sister paused in the doorway, shrouded by her white habit. She turned toward Karin and Kenta and smiled. "Goodbye. May peace and good fortune grace both of you."

Her emphasis on the word "both" bugged Karin, but before she could respond, the door closed and China was gone. She looked over at Kenta, who held his head in his hands and rocked gently back and forth.

"Are you going to write her, Kenta?"

"Regularly? Maybe a postcard every once in a while. I mean, stamps are kinda . . ." Kenta shook his head. His face was red, but his expression bore no trace of regret.

Karin couldn't keep the inevitable question bottled up any longer. "Weren't you in love with her?"

"Huh?" Kenta stopped rocking.

An awkward silence stretched between them. Karin realized she had to finish what she started. "It's just that you looked so happy when she came here the first time . . ."

"Of course I did! She brought my umbrella back! She even fixed it. She could have kept it forever, since I didn't know her address or anything. I had spent the whole day wondering how I could afford to buy a new one."

"Oh," Karin said simply. *So that was why he'd been in such a good mood. I was worried over nothing! Not that I was worried at all, of course . . .*

Anju and Maki had teased her about it so often that she had almost started to believe it was true. Karin smacked her forehead.

Kenta looked thoughtful. "Speaking of money, I picked up a bunch of coins outside the hospital. I guess I could buy a stamp with that . . ."

"Outside the hospital?" Karin practically pounced on him. "That's mine! My wallet came open when I got out of the car. How much did you find?"

"Four or five hundred yen. You can have it back if it's yours."

Karin welled up with happiness. "Thank god!"

She had already lost a wallet to a thieving girl at school just before summer vacation. And now with her tote and everything inside it having gone up in flames, she needed every yen she could find to replace her gear before the new term. At least her cell phone had been safely tucked away in the mother superior's car.

"At least my change made it out okay," she sniffed.

"Don't cry! Are things really that tight? Is that why you were trying to get more hours? I can give it back after work!" Kenta slipped a comforting arm around her shoulder.

"Really? I could spare a ten percent finder's fee . . ."

"Forget it. The way you look, how can I ask for that?"

"Really? Thanks!" Karin beamed at him.

Kenta scratched his cheek, embarrassed. "At least you're safe. That's the main thing. We're both safe. Forget the money. We were in a fire; we had a gun pointed at us. Hard to believe it all happened just last week."

As her friend spoke, Karin suddenly realized that they hadn't spoken directly about the events at the hospital. Karin and Kenta rarely had the same schedule at Julian, and when their shifts did line up, they were both too busy to talk about things.

"Sorry, Kenta. For running away and leaving you to explain everything . . ."

"I don't mind. It's not like your brother would let me do anything else without wiping my memories. I told the cops that I just happened to be walking by and heard their screams. They seemed to buy it," Kenta said.

He screwed up his eyes and looked at Karin. "But there's something I don't get. Weren't your fingerprints all over the scene? And what about the bits of your bag that survived the fire?"

"My brother said he used the bats to cover for me." Ren had left a few bats behind to keep an eye on things. Any police or firemen to discover trace evidence of his sister had their minds wiped on the way back to the station.

"If I'd said anything stupid, he'd have wiped my memory, too." Kenta folded his arms defensively.

"I doubt it," Karin cooed. "My brother wouldn't . . . Well, he might. Just a little. Huh. Anyway, don't worry."

"How can I not worry? Your brother and your mom are really scary."

"Sorry." Karin flushed with shame whenever she recalled how her family had threatened Kenta after he discovered her vampiric nature.

"There's nothing for you to apologize for," Kenta said sweetly. "Ren scared the crap out of me when he erased China's memory without even a warning. I guess it would have been bad if she'd remembered you biting her, but still . . ."

His words brought back memories of biting China. And more disturbingly, what happened afterward, the events China had described as merely a dream . . .

Karin looked at him hesitantly. "Thank you, Kenta, for defending me in front of China after everything she said to me."

"Anyone would have done it," he retorted, avoiding her gaze uncomfortably. "She was panicking. She didn't see the big picture. I can see why she would think what she did, not knowing about your situation. But I don't care if you're human or not. I never want to be the kind of person that would belittle someone like that."

Kenta ran a hand through his unruly hair. His life philosophy revolved around basic human decency.

Before anyone knew she was a vampire, Karin had suffered a series of explosive nosebleeds at school. Most of the boys had made fun of her for weeks. Kenta was alone in standing up for her and making sure she was okay.

Karin flashed a relieved smile.

Kenta met her gaze.

For a moment, neither could think of anything to say. A chorus of cicadas washed over the room, adding a surreal sheen to the scene.

Karin could feel her heart pounding. *Why is it beating so fast?*

"Usui! Maaka!" The manager waddled into view, baring his teeth in a troubled smile. "I hate to insist, but if your guest is gone, I could really use some extra hands in the dining room. You can exchange longing glances when you're finished with work."

"That's not what we were doing!"

"Absolutely not!"

Karin and Kenta shouted, but the manager was already gone.

A trickle of sweat rolled down Karin's face. *It was just a moment of silence! We weren't staring at each other! Honestly!*

She felt as if her body was going to catch fire. Kenta wouldn't meet her gaze. She stalked out the room purposefully. "Better get back to work!"

"Karin! Where are you going? Look out! In front of you!"

"Huh?" Karin had meant to run toward the dining room, but had turned the wrong way out of the storeroom. She slammed into the back door so forcefully it shook the building.

The ferry weighed nineteen tons, but cut through the water with ease.

China stood on the deck, gazing at the Inland Sea as the wind whipped through her habit. It was the first time she had been on a boat since camp in elementary school. The spray of saltwater pleased her. Islands and ships passed by, green and red and white against the beautiful blue of the ocean.

The ferry was still thirty minutes from the island.

China resolved to write letters to everyone she knew when she reached her destination. *Kenta. Karin. Ren—I won't write a letter to him. There's no need.*

She closed her eyes and put her fingers to her lips. A loving smile played across her face as she cast her mind across treasured memories. The night at the hospital was hazy. But although she'd told one thing to the police and another to her new friends, there was one other thing she'd remembered but kept to herself.

It was the memory of warm lips settling on her neck. A sudden pain, followed by an intangible sweetness. Platinum hair. Garnet eyes. A profile like a statue on the Saint Angelo bridge . . .

She felt no guilt. Touching Ren wasn't contact with a man. *It was a blessing from an angel.*

China believed it was a miracle. God's will given flesh and granted unto her.

She had been bound by her fear of fire ever since the conflagration of her youth. But at last she was free. No longer would she cry, paralyzed with fear.

She vaguely recalled putting the flames out with the fire extinguisher. The memories had the consistency of a dream. China believed they were given to her from above—sacred treasures not to be shared by anyone else.

China opened her eyes and looked out over the sea once more. Golden sunlight reflected off the water as if it was ablaze, but the imagery no longer startled her. The memory of putting out the hospital fire gave her confidence.

She determined to work hard at the new convent and become a model nun. China knew she could now bear any burden with both feet planted on the ground. She put her hands together and closed her eyes once more.

"Peace and good fortune to all . . ." she whispered.

Sunlight sparkled on the water; the sea winds grabbed her words and carried them far away.

Hi there! My name is Tohru Kai. Thanks for reading my book.

This is the second novel based on Yuna Kagesaki's manga *Karin*, which is enjoying a successful monthly run in *Dragon Edge*. Like the first book, this one can be read independently of the manga but offers something extra for fans of the series.

Shortly after the events of the first novel, Kenta Usui discovered Karin's true nature and squared off against her family before reaching a shaky truce. This book breezes through those details because they were already explored in the manga. Be sure to check it out if you want to know more about this gripping turn of events.

Most of you have probably already read the manga and want to know where this story fits in. It takes place over a few days before the upcoming third volume. Talk about perfect timing—you can read this book while you wait for that one!

I know, I know. That was basically the same thing I wrote in the first volume. I should probably write something new. Last time I got a little excited and maybe crossed the line. Sorry about that!

Nah, I take it back. What's wrong with admitting I like cute girls? It's fun to write about cute girls!

This book was a blast to write. Two girls as main characters! Karin and the novice sister. I did say I love writing about cute girls, didn't I?

Why a nun?

Because habits are hot, of course.

But here's the problem. I know next to nothing about Christianity and have no idea what real nuns are like. I checked online and read a few books, but information on the daily routine was too basic for coverage—the same way cookbooks don't tell you how to cook rice. I asked a nearby convent for a tour, but they declined. Instead, they helpfully answered some questions over the phone.

A lot of the details in this book come from my friend Eko, who used to go to church. Thanks for listening to all my questions! I only managed to get this book finished in time because of you.

But some of you probably know a lot more about the lives of nuns than myself. Some of you might even *be* nuns! Please remember that this is a work of fiction. (That should get me out of trouble!) If you find any errors, send them to my editors.

I did make one deliberate error. The nuns in this book are oddly early to rise. I had no choice; there was no other way to bring the characters together. The book is set during the long daylight hours of

July. I needed the nuns awake during the darkness so that the other vampire characters could move around. Karin is unique in tolerating daylight.

I had a great time writing *Chibi Vampire: The Novel, Volume 2*. I hope you enjoyed reading it! We're not sure if there will be a third volume yet. There are signs of movement in the editorial department. Maybe I'll be able to write a tomboy into it. Or maybe it's time to get to know Karin's father?

At any rate, if there's a third volume, be sure to pick it up!

Finally, I'd like to thank the original author and illustrator, Yuna Kagesaki. And of course my editor!

Thanks to everyone involved in the production of this book, Fujimi Mystery, and the editors of *Dragon Edge*.

And thanks to all of my readers!

Tohru Kai
www.ocn.zaq.ne.jp/kai-tohru/

—2004 February (The afternoon I went out without an umbrella and it rained)

Check out the following series
also available from TOKYOPOP Fiction:

POP
FICTION